WALT WHITMAN

LI

OAK, WITH MOSS

Art by BRIAN SELZNICK

Afterword by Karen Karbiener

Abrams ComicArts
New York

ELEVE (*noun*): student, pupil. From the French.

In 2004 I befriended the legendary children's book author and illustrator Maurice Sendak, and we got to know each other through a series of late-night phone calls. I had just finished a children's book about Walt Whitman, and by coincidence Maurice was reading *Leaves of Grass* for the first time. During one of our conversations, Maurice shared a story he'd learned from his friend the scholar Hershel Parker. In the 1850s Whitman had written a cycle of twelve poems called "Live Oak, with Moss," which Maurice described as a love story between two men who eventually part.

Whitman never published the cycle. Instead he cut them up, rearranged them, and hid them in the "Calamus" cluster of poems in the 1860 edition of *Leaves of Grass.* They remained completely unknown for a hundred years until they were discovered and extracted in the 1950s by bibliographer Fredson Bowers. Hershel Parker had written about these poems, and he wanted Maurice to illustrate "Live Oak, with Moss," which had not yet been introduced to the general public. Even though Maurice made it clear he never illustrated poems because "poems don't need illustrations," he was still tempted to take this project on. In my diary that night I wrote: *I really hope he does! I want to see it!*

I'm sorry we'll never see what Maurice would have made of these poems, but I couldn't get them out of my mind. And then a few years ago, my friend Karen Karbiener suggested I create my own book from "Live Oak, with Moss" in honor of Walt Whitman's two-hundredth birthday. But how could I illustrate poems when Maurice Sendak himself had said poems should not be illustrated? The book you now hold in your hands is my answer. The drawings here aren't meant to be illustrations of the poems but a framework, or a lens, through which they can be discovered. I hope Maurice would have approved. This book is dedicated to his memory and his inspiration, with all my love.

—Brian Selznick

LIVE OAK,
WITH MOSS

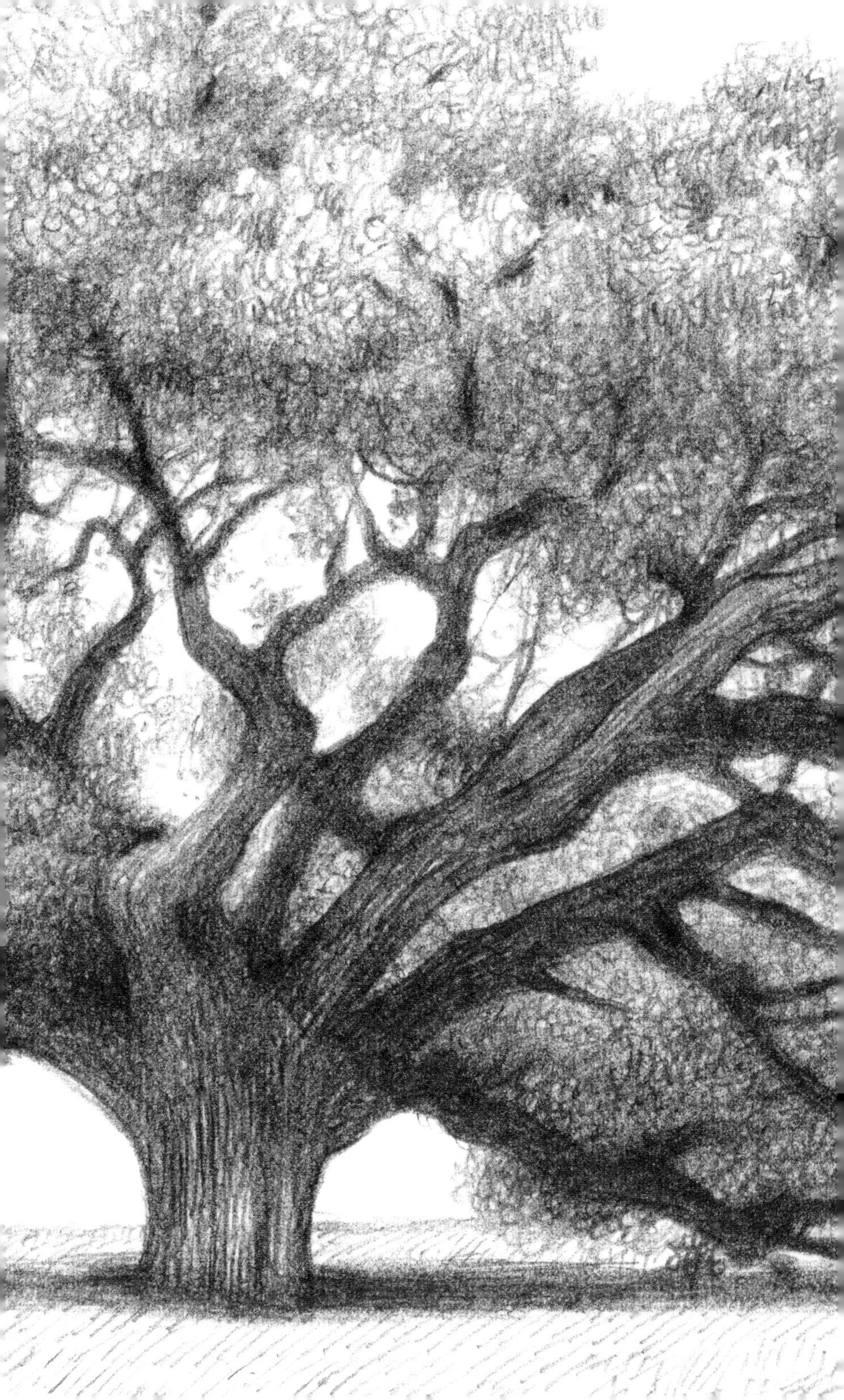

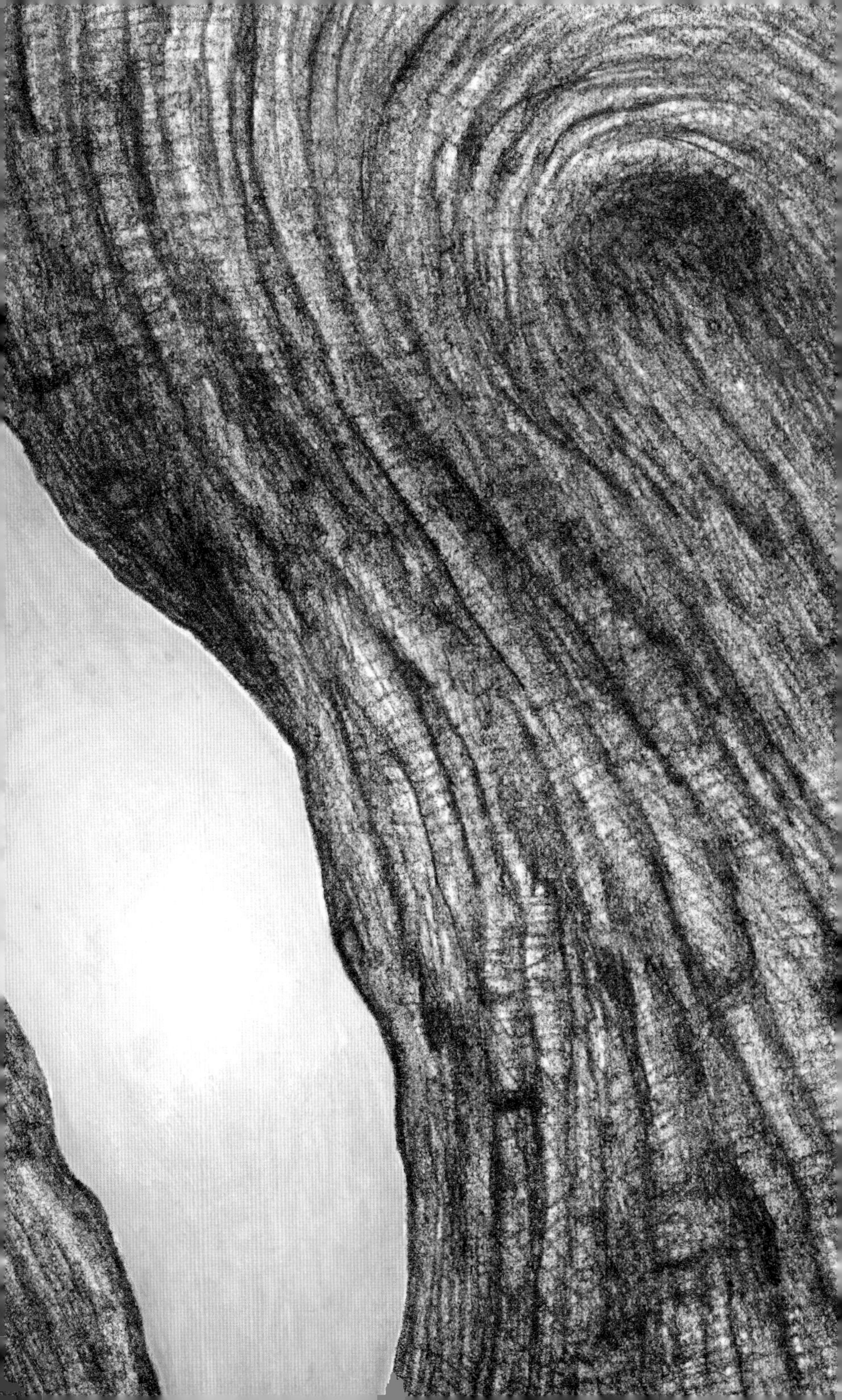

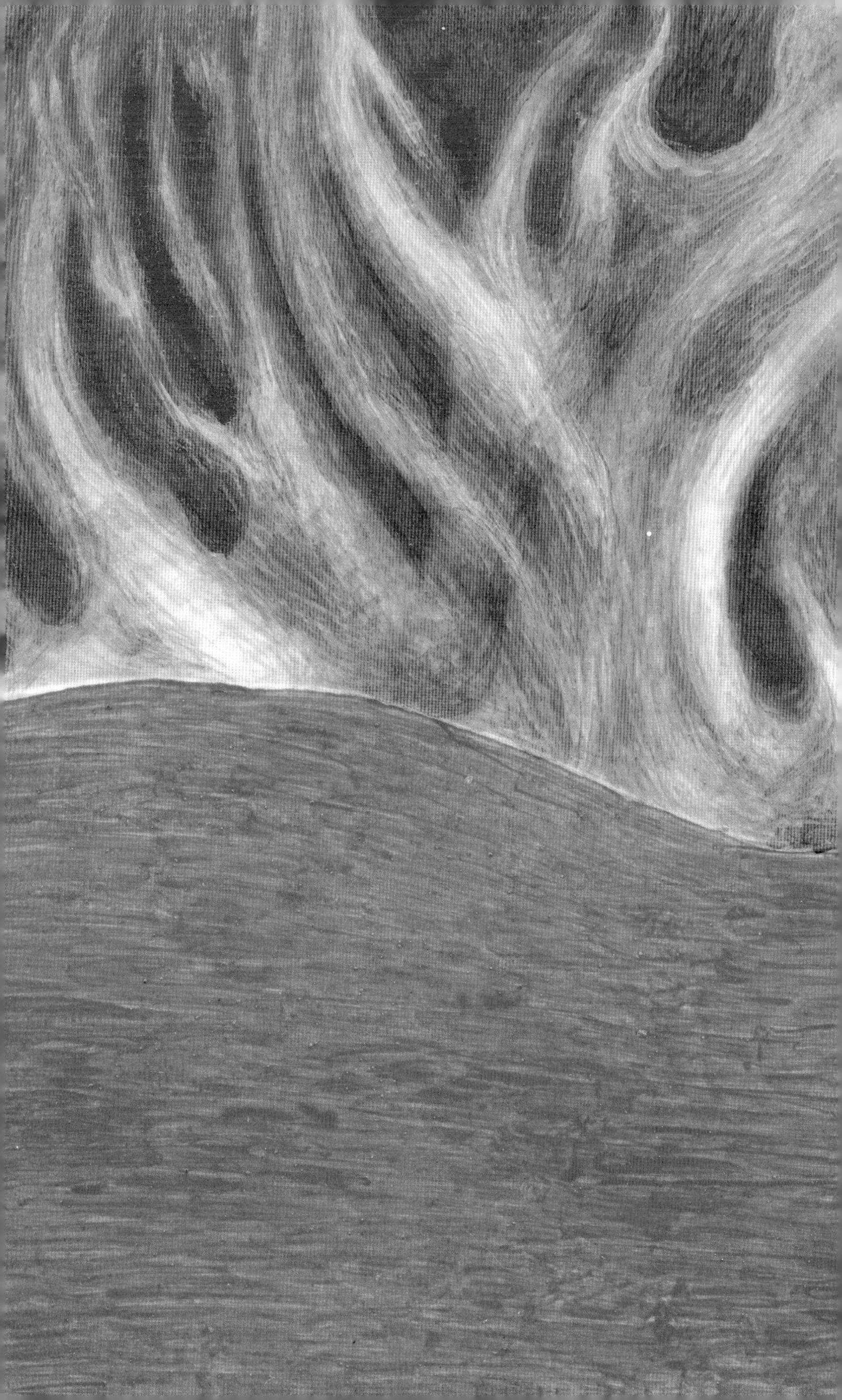

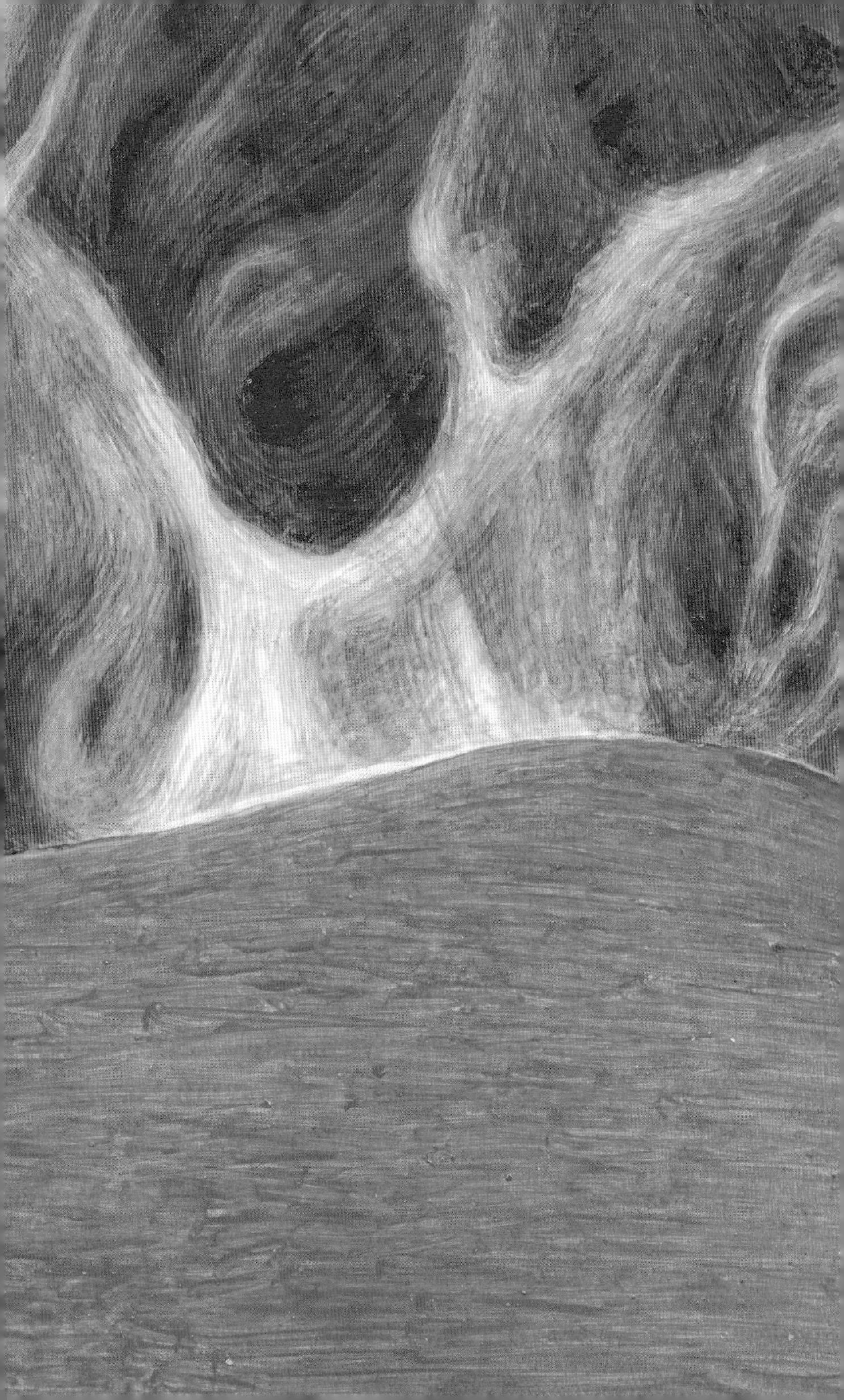

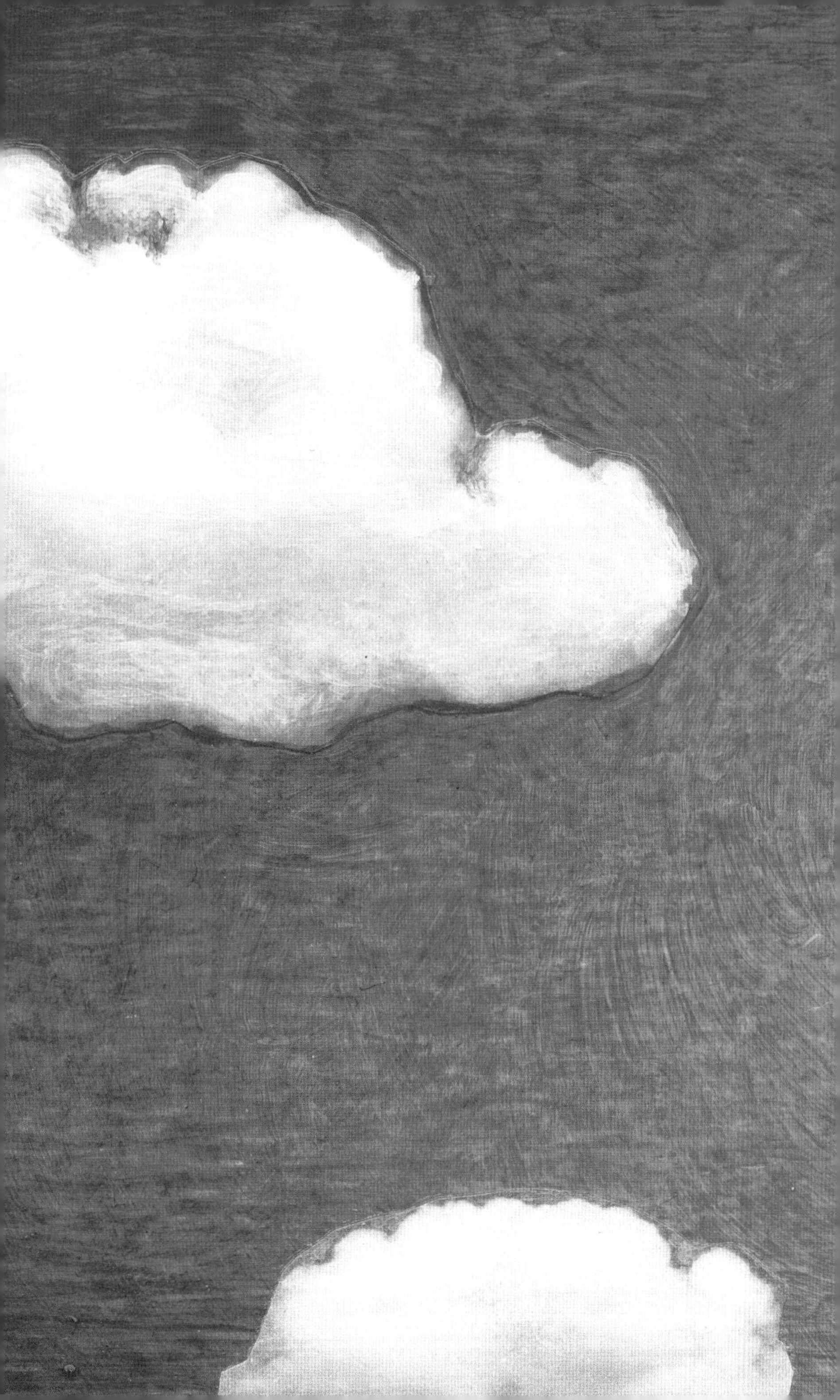

MANUFACTORY.
PATENT FI
RKS and
JONES' PATENT BA
FACTORY.
BANK VAULTS &
MARBLEIZED IRON DEPOT

N G S F A C T O R Y.
& BURGLAR PROOF SAFES.
& HALLS' PATENT POWDER PROOF LOCKS.
ULT DOORS and CHILLD IRON SAFES.
BROADWAY.
SALE ROOMS for SAFES and

RED MUNROE & CO.
OLESALE & RETAIL.
LINCOLN & THOMPSON
ANO FORTES
PARIS
STRAW & FA
WARE
HARDW
CLOTHING 441

ONUMENTS, STATUAR

GAS FIXTURES.
FURNITURE
GENERAL.
FRENCH
HOUSE
PARIS
RUE
CAUMARTIN
RINGUET-LEPRINCE, MARCOTTE
341 HYDRAULICS
BRANCHES
HOUSE
ARD,

GURNEY.
PLATED WARES.
PENDANTS,
BRACKETS,

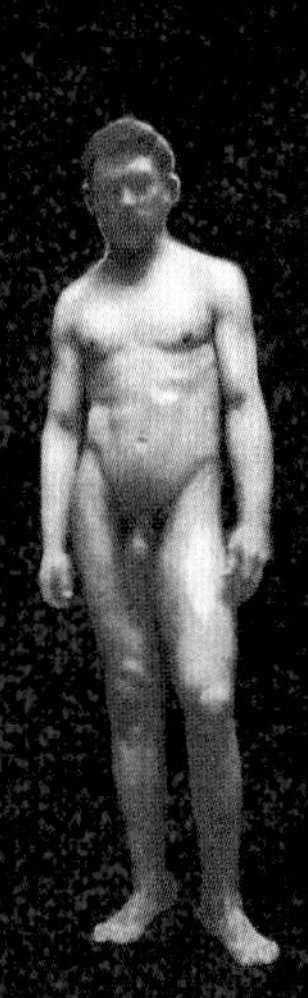

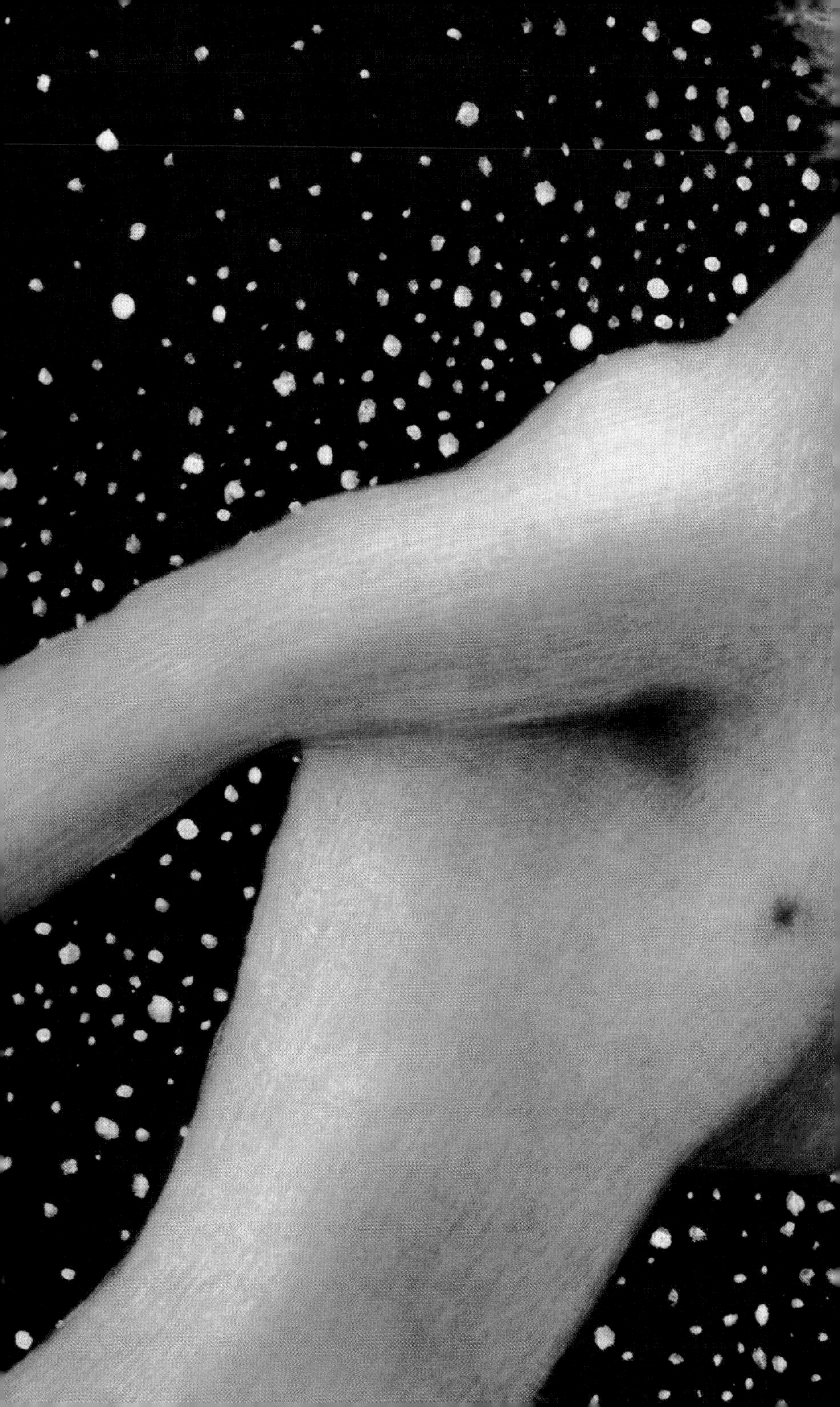

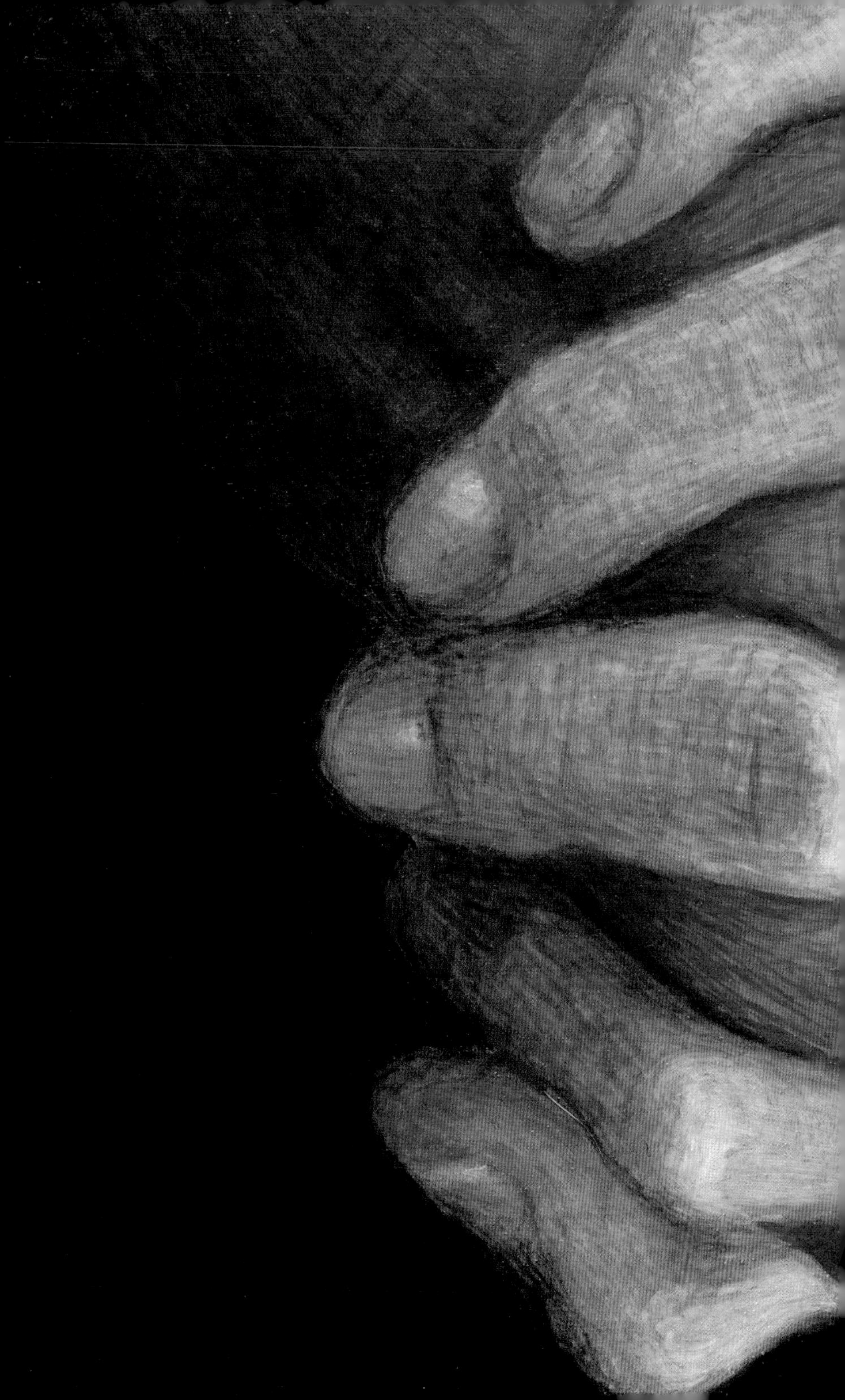

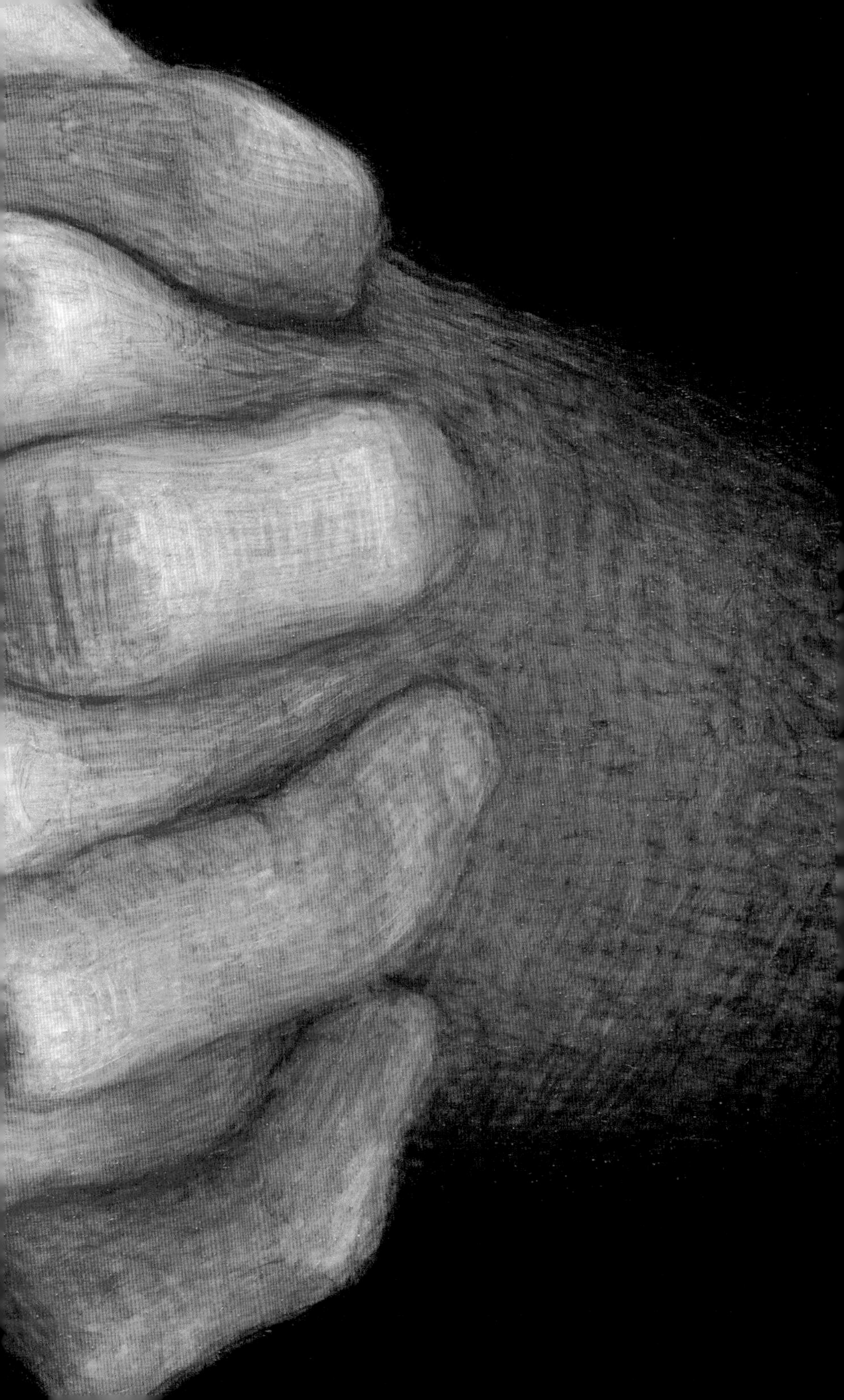

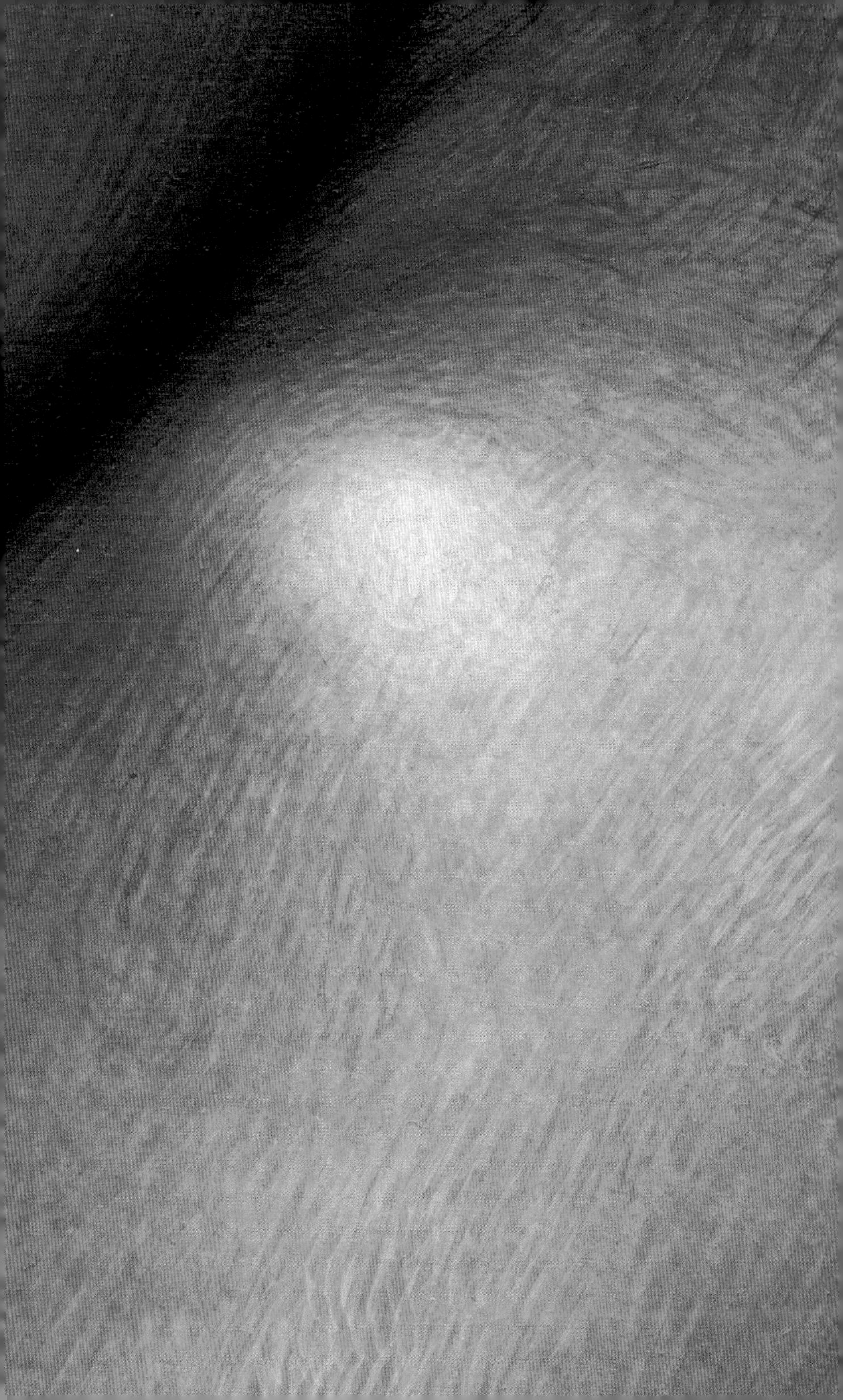

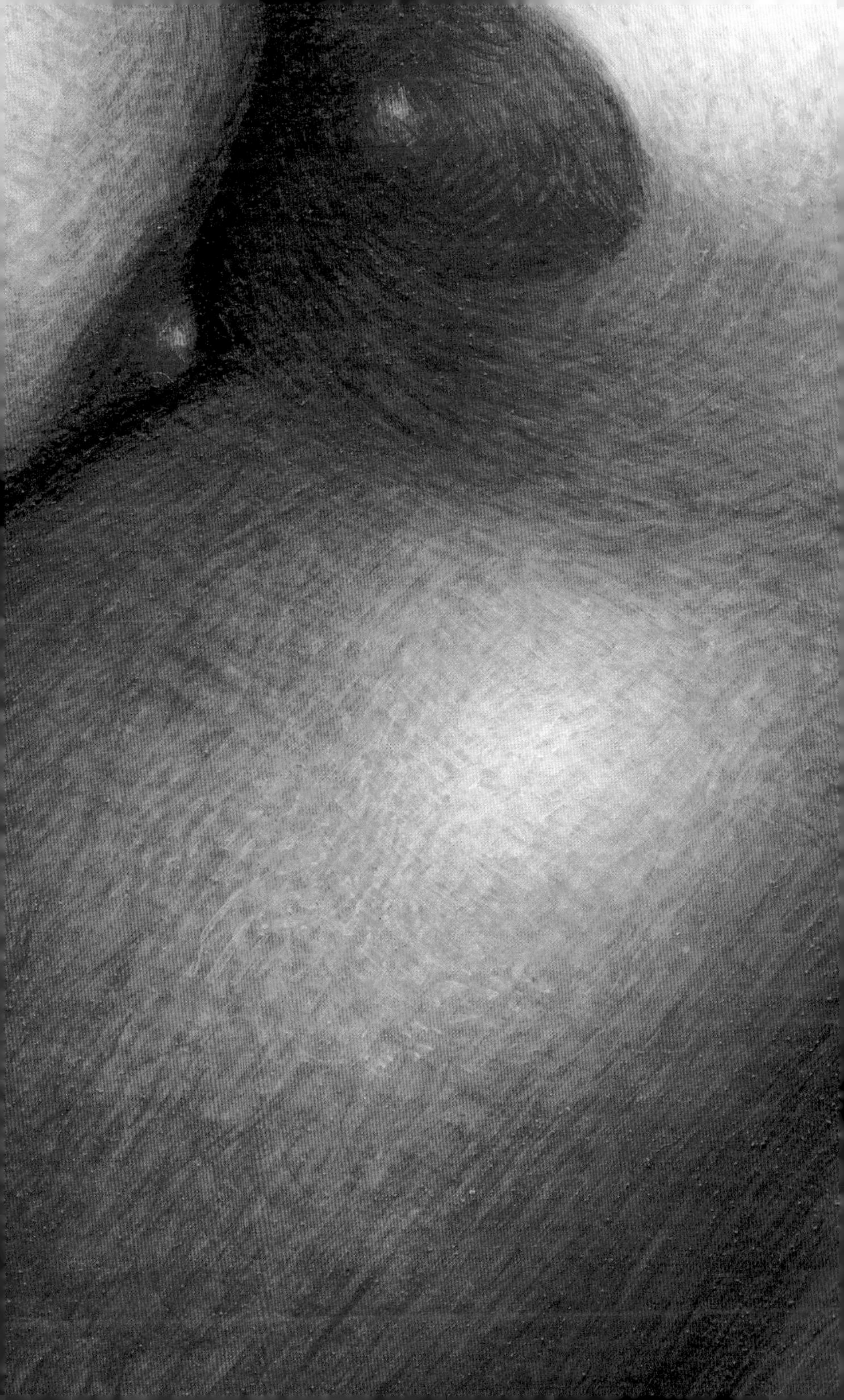

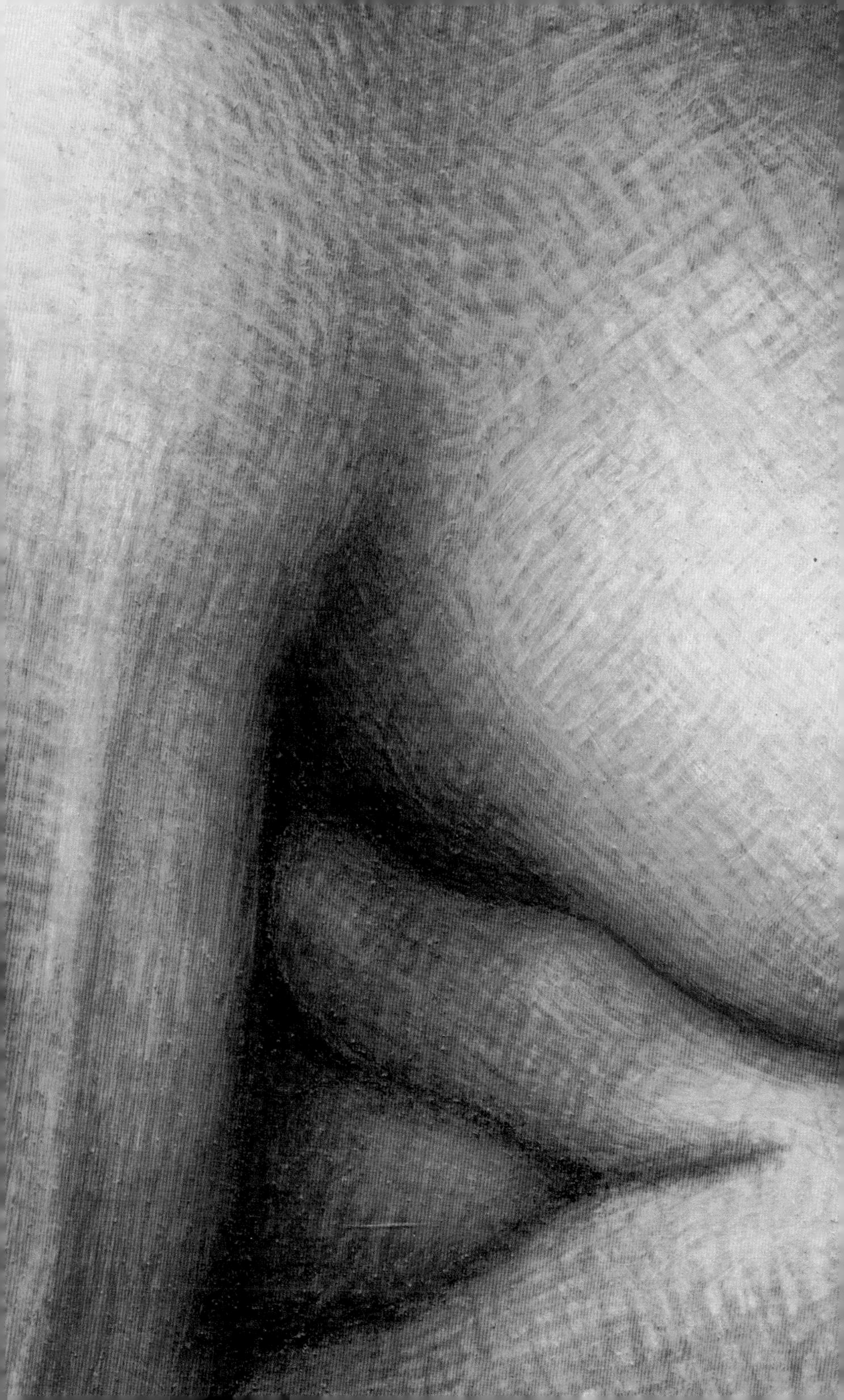

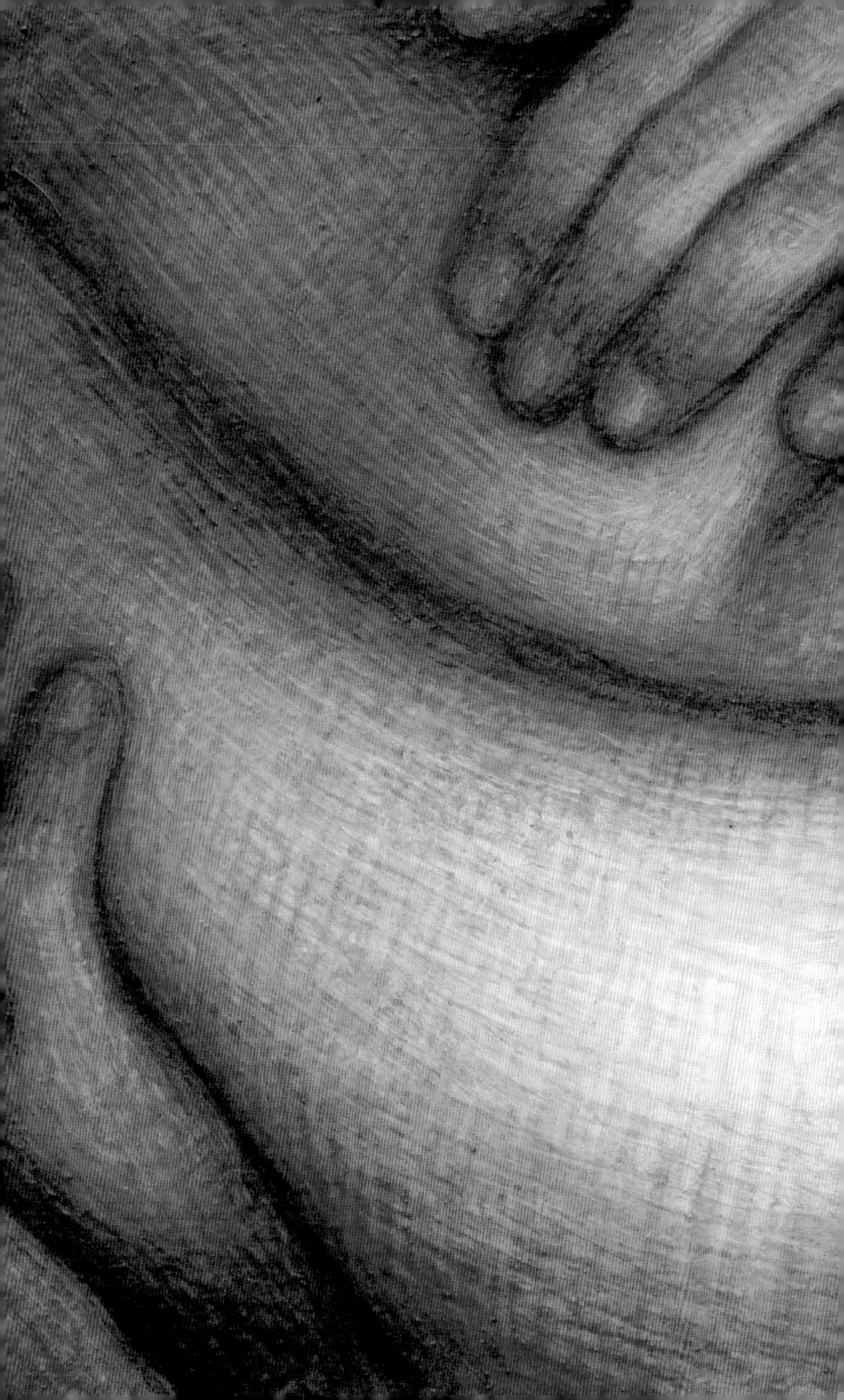

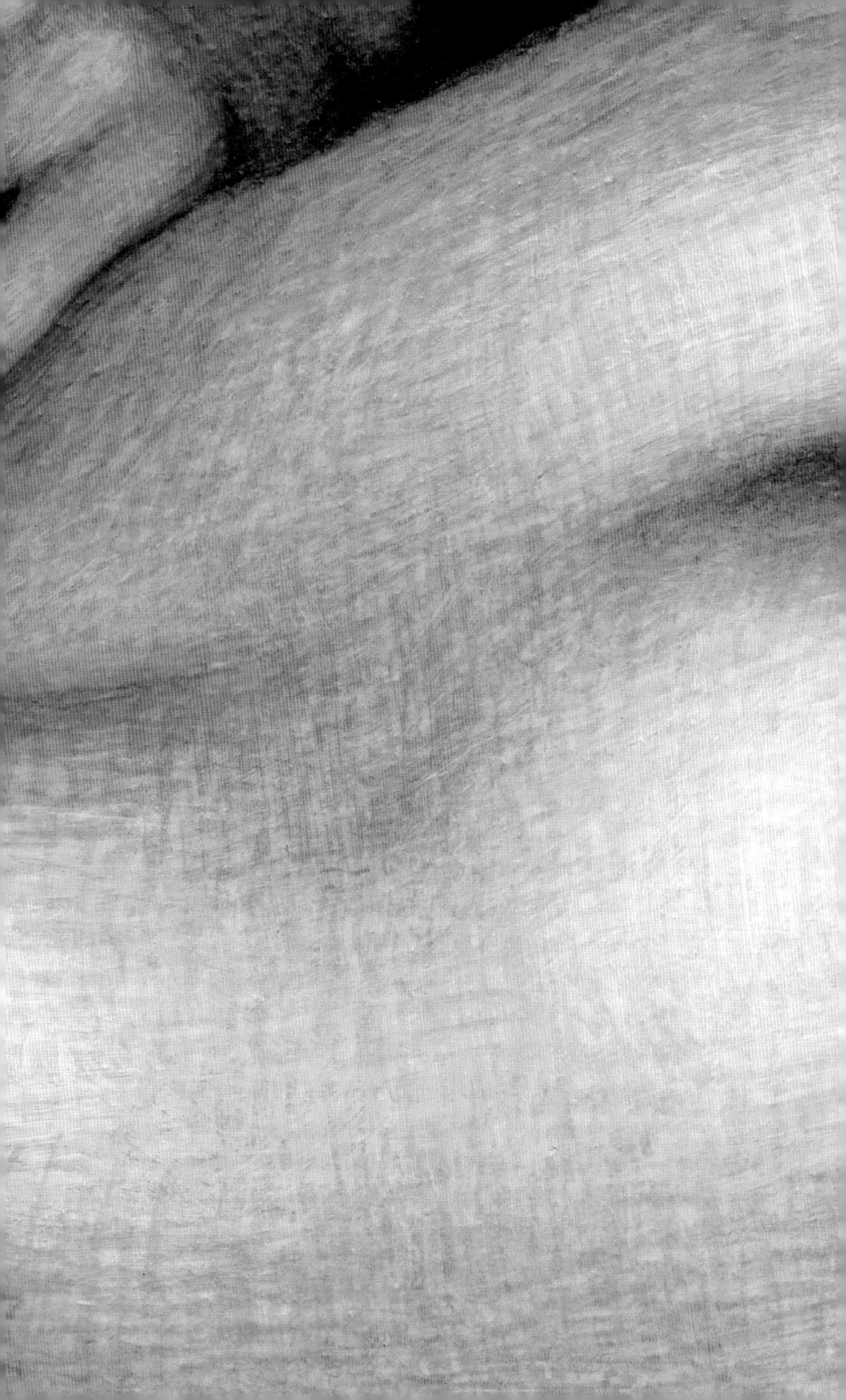

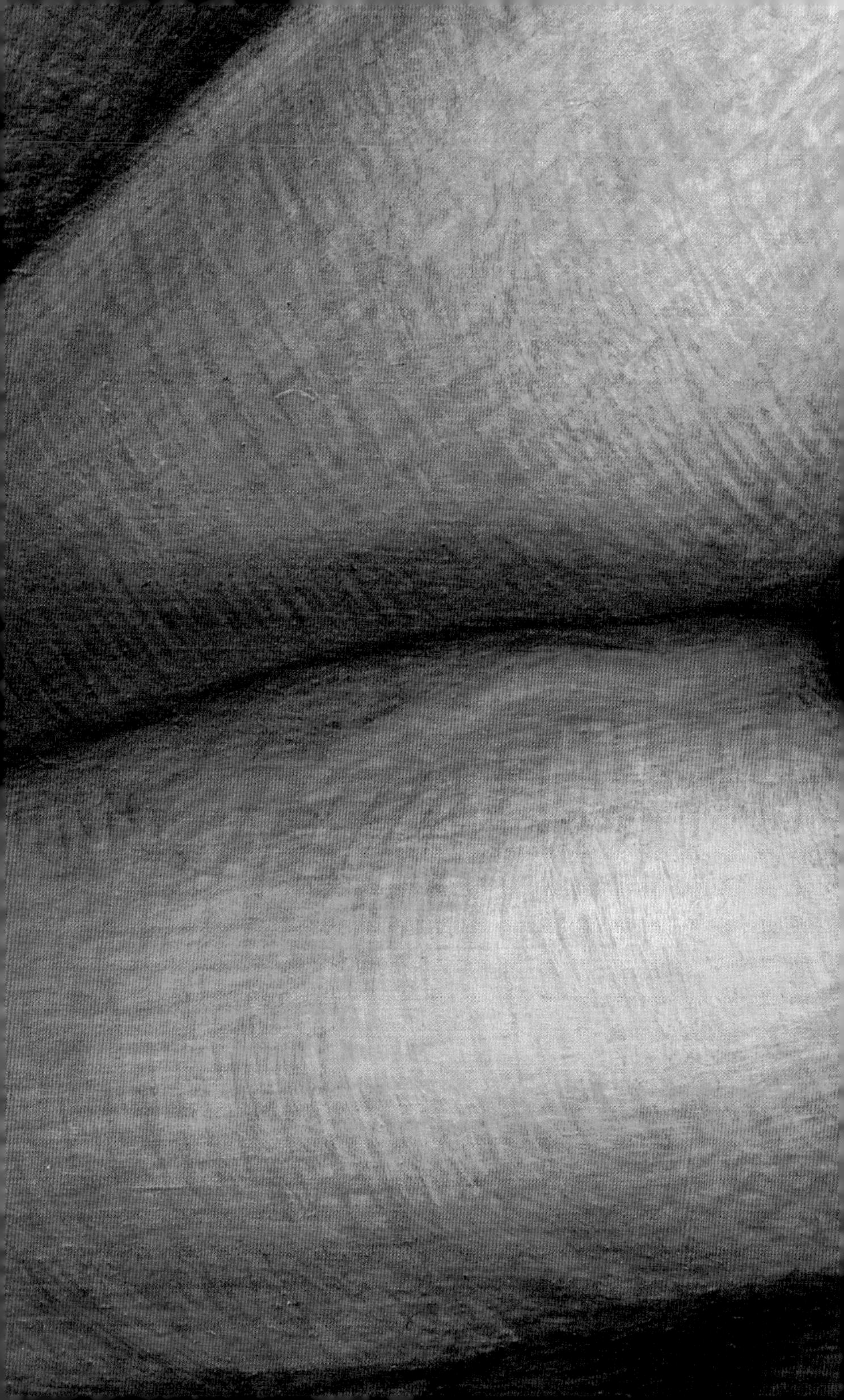

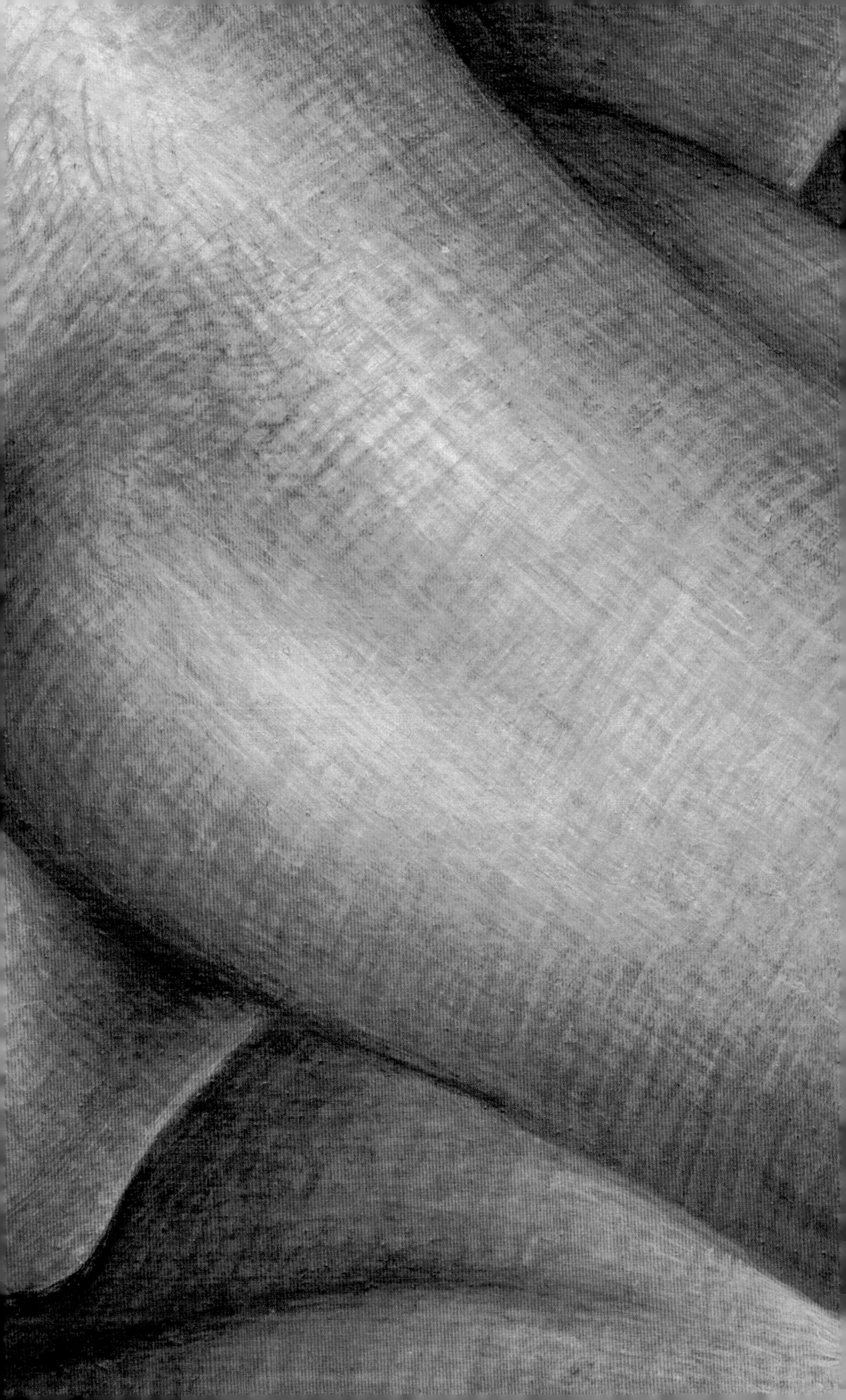

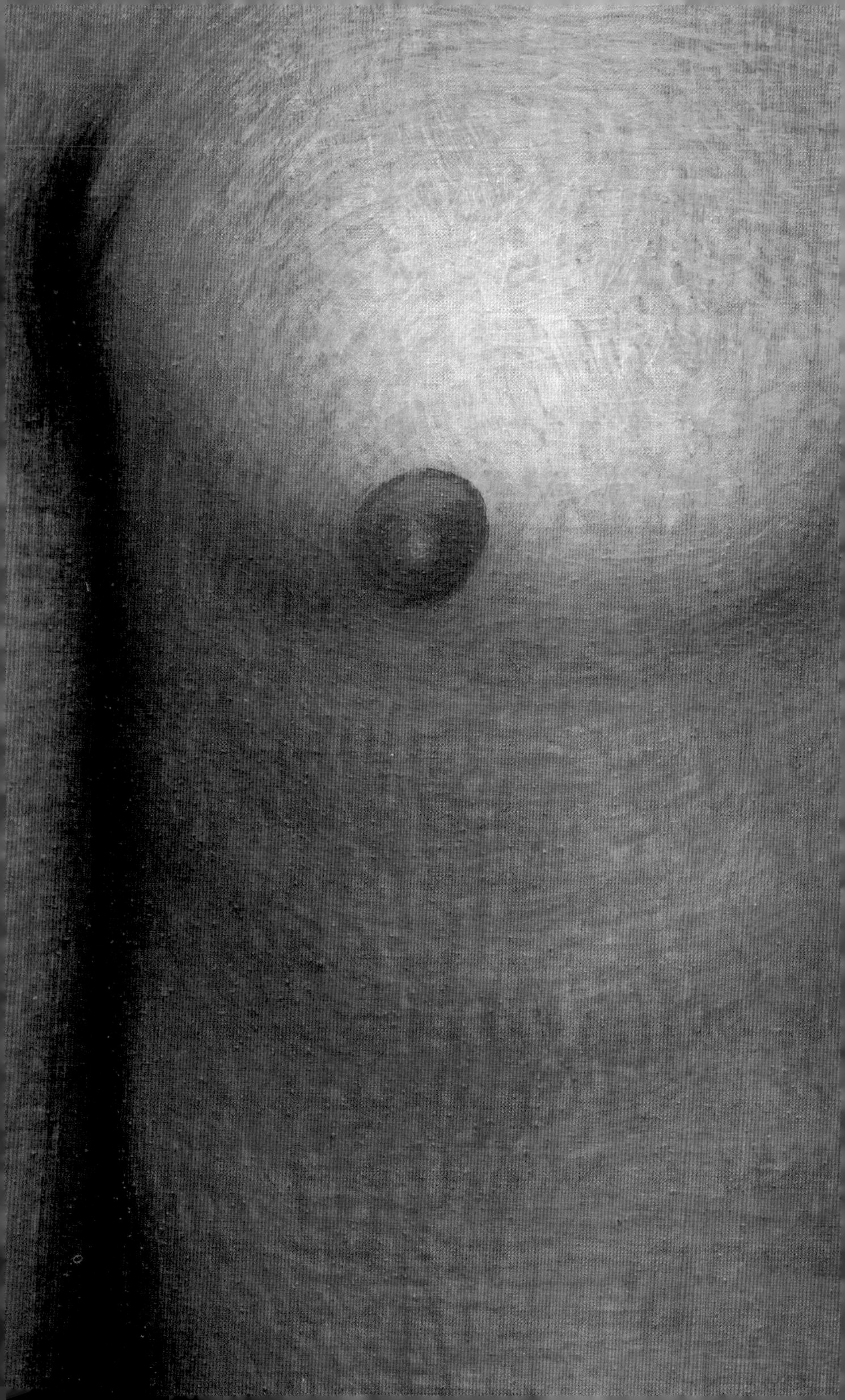

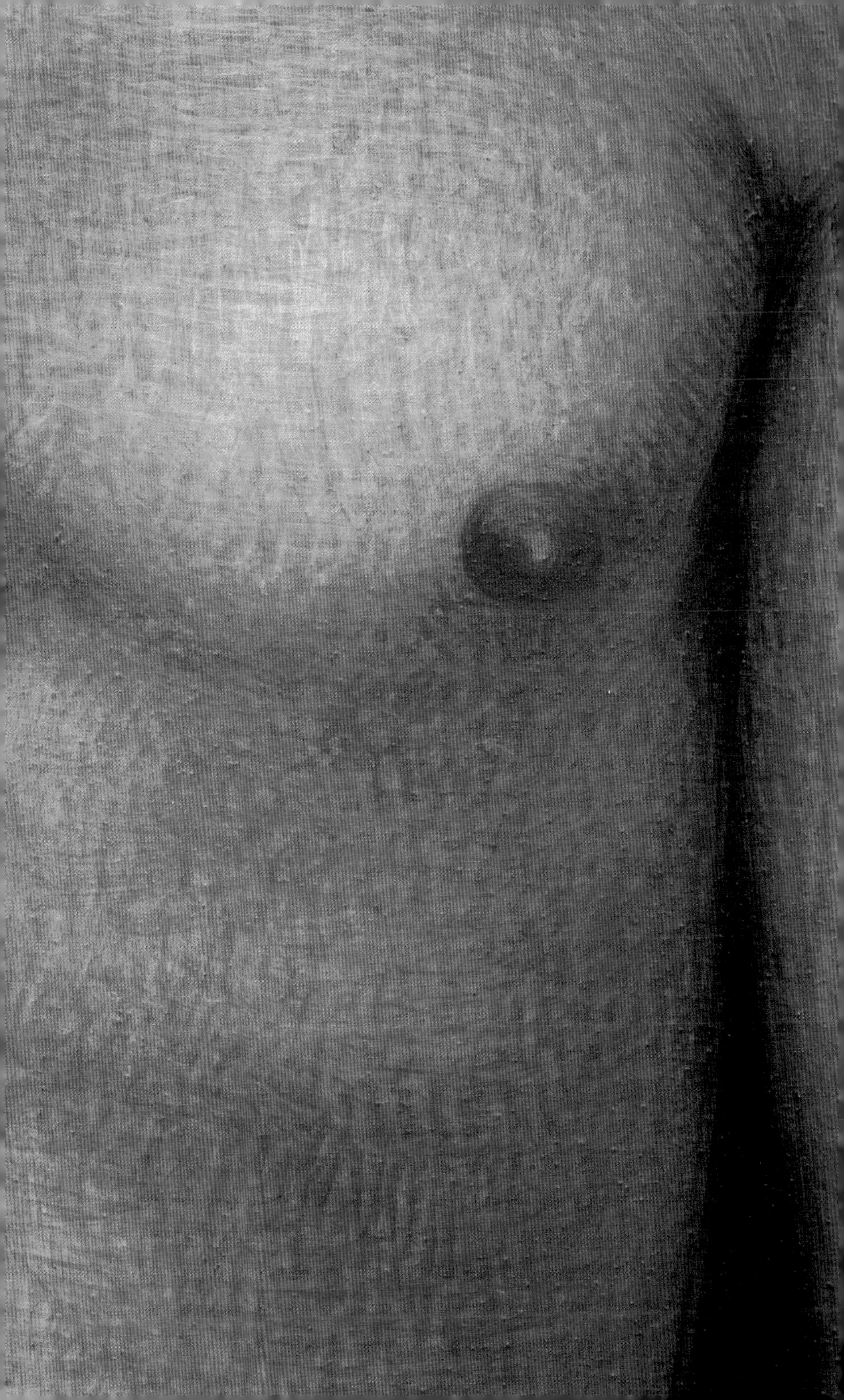

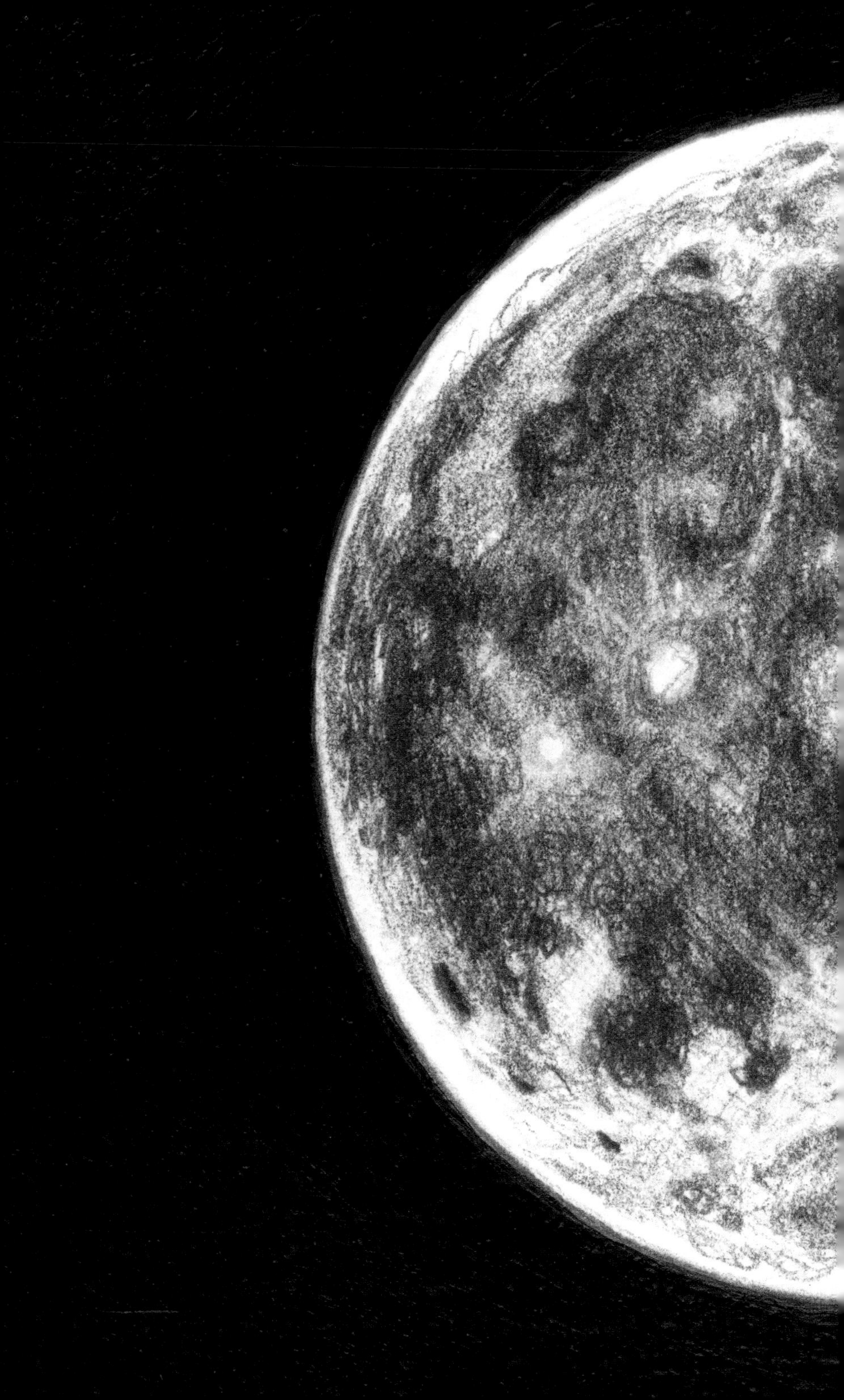

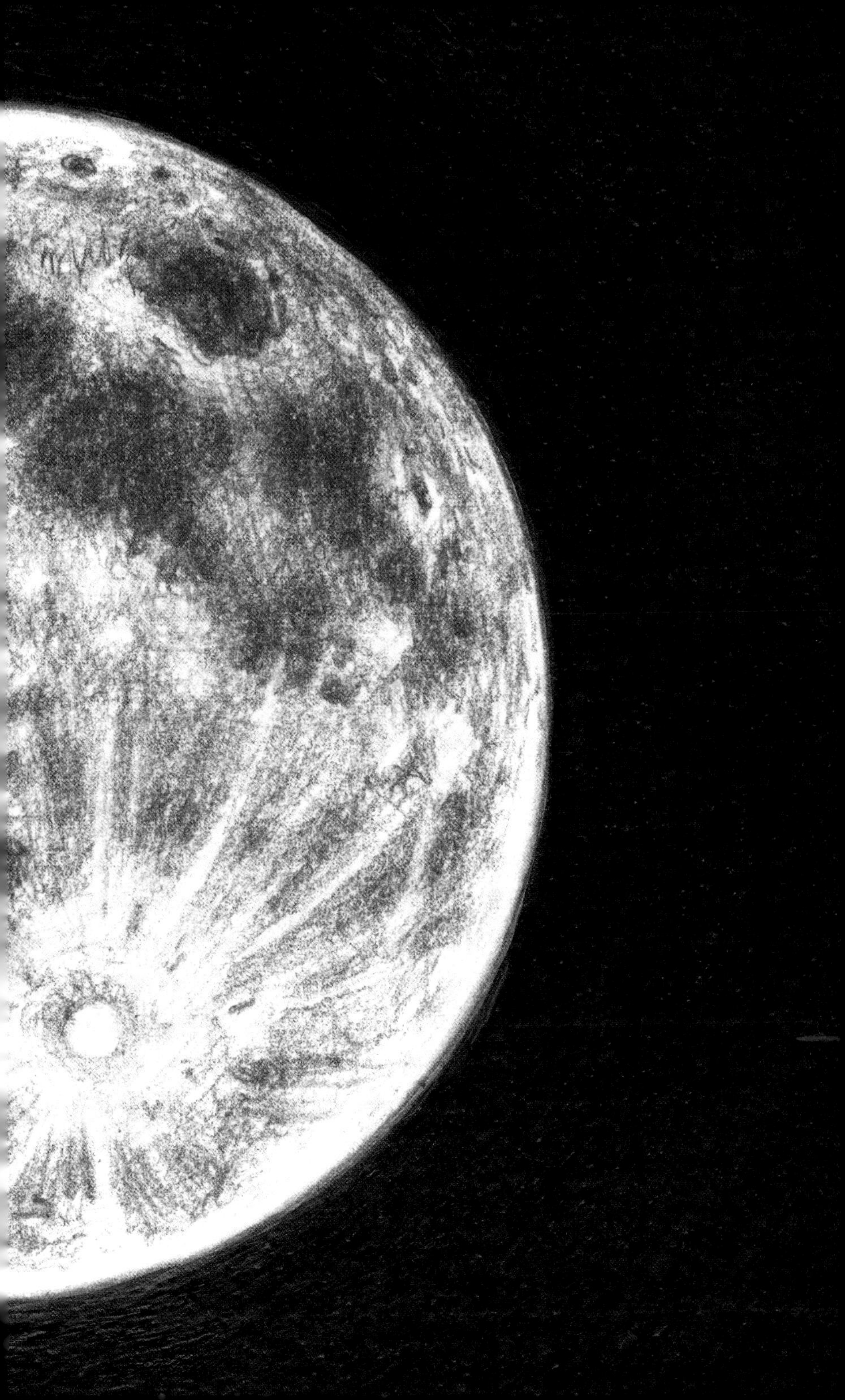

I.

Not the heat flames up and consumes,
Not the sea-waves hurry in and out,
Not the air, delicious and dry, the air of the ripe summer, bears lightly along white down-balls of myriads of seeds, wafted, sailing gracefully, to drop where they may,
Not these—O none of these, more than the flames of me, consuming, burning for his love whom I love—O none, more than I, hurrying in and out;
Does the tide hurry, seeking something, and never give up?—O I, the same, to seek my life-long lover;
O nor down-balls, nor perfumes, nor the high rain-emitting clouds, are borne through the open air, more than my copious soul is borne through the open air, wafted in all directions, for friendship, for love.—

II.

I saw in Louisiana a live-oak growing,
All alone stood it, and the moss hung down from
the branches,
Without any companion it grew there, glistening
out with joyous leaves of dark green,
And its look, rude, unbending, lusty, made me think
of myself;
But I wondered how it could utter joyous leaves,
standing alone there without its friend, its
lover—For I knew I could not;
And I plucked a twig with a certain number of
leaves upon it, and twined around it a little
moss, and brought it away—And I have
placed it in sight in my room,
It is not needed to remind me as of my friends, (for
I believe lately I think of little else than of
them,)
Yet it remains to me a curious token—I write these
pieces, and name them after it;
For all that, and though the live oak glistens there
in Louisiana, solitary in a wide flat space,
uttering joyous leaves all its life, without
a friend, a lover, near—I know very well I
could not.

III.

When I heard at the close of the day how I had been praised in the Capitol, still it was not a happy night for me that followed;
And else, when I caroused—Or when my plans were accomplished—it was well enough—Still I was not happy;
But the day when I rose at dawn from the bed of perfect health, electric, inhaling sweet breath,
When I saw the full moon in the west grow pale and disappear in the morning light,
When I wandered alone over the beach, and undressing, bathed, laughing with the waters, and saw the sun rise,
And when I thought how my friend, my lover, was coming, then I was happy;
O then each breath tasted sweeter—and all that day my food nourished me more—And the beautiful day passed well,
And the next came with equal joy—And with the next, at evening, came my friend,
And that night, O you happy waters, I heard you beating the shores—But my heart beat happier than you—for he I love was returned and sleeping by my side,
And that night in the stillness his face was inclined toward me, while the moon's clear beams shone,
And his arm lay lightly over my breast—And that night I was happy.

IV.

This moment as I sit alone, yearning and pensive, it seems to me there are other men, in other lands, yearning and pensive.
It seems to me I can look over and behold them, in Germany, France, Spain—Or far away in China, or in Russia—talking other dialects,
And it seems to me if I could know those men better I should love them as I love men in my own lands,
It seems to me they are as wise, beautiful, benevolent, as any in my own lands;
O I know we should be brethren—I know I should be happy with them.

V.

Long I thought that knowledge alone would suffice
me—O if I could but obtain knowledge!
Then my lands engrossed me—For them I would
live—I would be their orator;
Then I met the examples of old and new heroes—I
heard the examples of warriors, sailors, and
all dauntless persons—And it seemed to me
I too had it in me to be as dauntless as any,
and would be so;
And then to finish all, it came to me to strike up the
songs of the New World—And then I
believed my life must be spent in singing;
But now take notice, Land of the prairies, Land of
the south savannas, Ohio's land,
Take notice, you Kanuck woods—and you, Lake
Huron—and all that with you roll toward
Niagara—and you Niagara also,

And you, Californian mountains—that you all find some one else that he be your singer of songs,
For I can be your singer of songs no longer—I have passed ahead—I have ceased to enjoy them.
I have found him who loves me, as I him, in perfect love,
With the rest I dispense—I sever from all that I thought would suffice me, for it does not—it is now empty and tasteless to me,
I heed knowledge, and the grandeur of The States, and the examples of heroes, no more,
I am indifferent to my own songs—I am to go with him I love, and he is to go with me,
It is to be enough for each of us that we are together—We never separate again.—

VI.

What think you I have taken my pen to record?
Not the battle-ship, perfect-model'd, majestic, that I
saw to day arrive in the offing, under full sail,
Nor the splendors of the past day—nor the
splendors of the night that envelopes me—
Nor the glory and growth of the great city
spread around me,

But the two men I saw to-day on the pier, parting
the parting of dear friends.
The one to remain hung on the other's neck and
passionately kissed him—while the one to
depart tightly prest the one to remain in his
arms.

VII.

You bards of ages hence! when you refer to me,
mind not so much my poems,
Nor speak of me that I prophesied of The States and
led them the way of their glories,
But come, I will inform you who I was underneath
that impassive exterior—I will tell you what
to say of me,
Publish my name and hang up my picture as that of
the tenderest lover,
The friend, the lover's portrait, of whom his friend,
his lover, was fondest,
Who was not proud of his songs, but of the
measureless ocean of love within him—and
freely poured it forth,
Who often walked lonesome walks thinking of his
dearest friends, his lovers,
Who pensive, away from one he loved, often lay
sleepless and dissatisfied at night,
Who, dreading lest the one he loved might after all
be indifferent to him, felt the sick feeling—
O sick! sick!
Whose happiest days were those, far away through
fields, in woods, on hills, he and another,
wandering hand in hand, they twain, apart
from other men.
Who ever, as he sauntered the streets, curved with
his arm the manly shoulder of his friend—
while the curving arm of his friend rested
upon him also.

VIII.

Hours continuing long, sore and heavy-hearted,
Hours of the dusk, when I withdraw to a lonesome and unfrequented spot, seating myself, leaning my face in my hands,
Hours sleepless, deep in the night, when I go forth, speeding swiftly the country roads, or through the city streets, or pacing miles and miles, stifling plaintive cries,
Hours discouraged, distracted,—For he, the one I cannot content myself without—soon I saw him content himself without me,
Hours when I am forgotten—(O weeks and months are passing, but I believe I am never to forget!)
Sullen and suffering hours—(I am ashamed—but it is useless—I am what I am;)
Hours of my torment—I wonder if other men ever have the like, out of the like feelings?
Is there even one other like me—distracted—his friend, his lover, lost to him?
Is he too as I am now? Does he still rise in the morning, dejected, thinking who is lost to him? And at night, awaking, think who is lost?
Does he too harbor his friendship silent and endless? Harbor his anguish and passion?
Does some stray reminder, or the casual mention of a name, bring the fit back upon him, taciturn and deprest?
Does he see himself reflected in me? In these hours does he see the face of his hours reflected?

IX.

I dreamed in a dream of a city where all the men
were like brothers,
O I saw them tenderly love each other—I often
saw them, in numbers, walking hand in
hand;
I dreamed that was the city of robust friends—
Nothing was greater there than the quality
of manly love—it led the rest,
It was seen every hour in the actions of the men of
that city, and in all their looks and words.—

X.

O you whom I often and silently come where you
 are, that I may be with you,
As I walk by your side, or sit near, or remain in the
 same room with you,
Little you know the subtle electric fire that for your
 sake is playing within me.—

XI.

Earth! My likeness! Though you look so impassive,
ample and spheric there,—I now suspect
that is not all,
I now suspect there is something terrible in you,
ready to break forth,
For an athlete loves me,—and I him—But toward
him there is something fierce and terrible in
me,
I dare not tell it in words—not even in these songs.

XII.

To the young man, many things to absorb, to
engraft, to develope, I teach, that he be my
eleve,
But if through him rolls not the blood of divine
friendship, hot and red—If he be not
silently selected by lovers, and do not silently
select lovers—of what use were it for him to
seek to become eleve of mine?

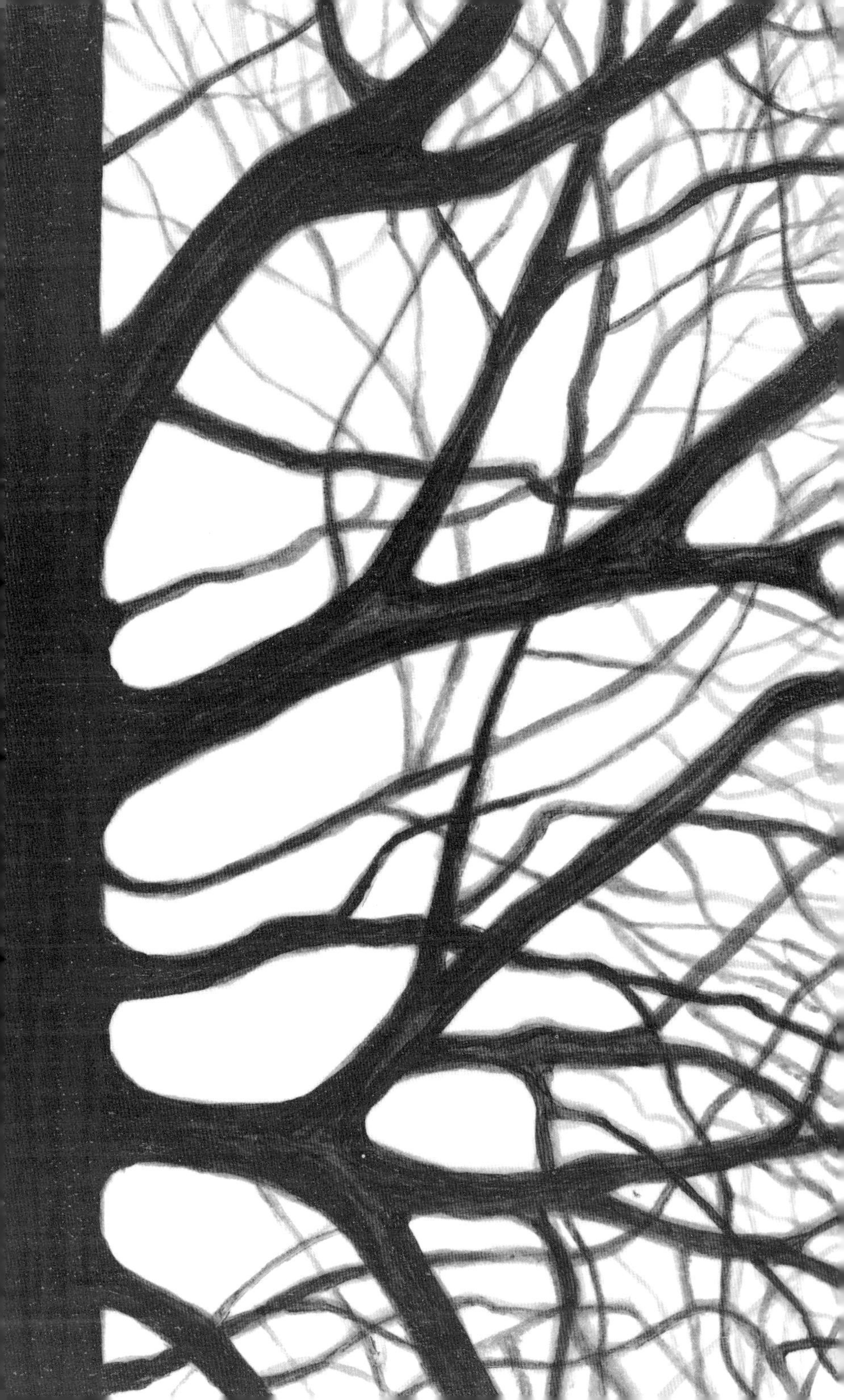

THE END

AFTERWORD

REMEMBER NOW REMEMBER THEN

As he was turning forty, Walt Whitman worked on twelve poems in a small handmade notebook he entitled "Live Oak, with Moss." He later took the book apart, edited these poems and intermixed them with thirty-three new poems to create the "Calamus" cluster of the third edition of *Leaves of Grass*. Whitman never published the "Live Oak, with Moss" poems as he had written them in his notebook, and there is no record of his mention of them to even his closest friends.

The disbanded leaves of the twelve original "Live Oak, with Moss" poems were discovered by scholar Fredson Bowers, who published their contents in the scholarly journal *Studies in Bibliography* in 1953. But the poems did not gain serious critical attention from academics until the 1990s. Even now, more than one hundred sixty years after Whitman conceived the idea of "Live Oak, with Moss," this revolutionary, extraordinarily beautiful and passionate cluster of poems remains largely unknown to the general public.

Yet they have immediate and powerful relevance for every reader who opens this book. For Whitman these poems were his first intense, sustained reflections on the love and attraction he felt for other men. For scholars they represent a new chapter in literary and social history. In these dozen poems, Whitman attempts to establish a definition of same-sex love decades before the word "homosexual" was in common parlance, and he dreams of a supportive community of lovers more than one hundred years before today's LGBTQ rights movement. Whether or not you know him and his work, whatever your sexual orientation and gender, you will find in these poems the timeless and courageous voice of a person attempting to be true to himself, body and soul. As we push open doors and start up conversations in this earnest, if conflicted, era, Whitman's reassembled and newly interpreted "Live Oak, with Moss" serves as a personal guidebook and a source of inspiration.

THE SEEDS

The second of eight children born to barely literate, financially unstable parents, Walter Whitman Jr. was a grammar school dropout who learned to love language while setting type for Brooklyn's booming print industry. The "signal event of my life up to that time," he writes in his prose memoir, *Specimen Days*, was gaining access to the Brooklyn Apprentice's Library, the city's first free circulating library.

Whitman must have felt at home in its collection of classic literature, travel, and geography books: in the library's tenth year and Whitman's sixteenth, he was recorded as "acting librarian" of its twelve hundred volumes. His self-led great books curriculum gave the budding poet something to shout about. "While living in Brooklyn, (1836–'50)," he continues in *Specimen Days*, "I went regularly every week in the mild seasons down to Coney island [*sic*], at that time a long, bare unfrequented shore, which I had all to myself, and where I loved, after bathing, to race up and down the hard sand, and declaim Homer or Shakspere [*sic*] to the surf and sea-gulls by the hour." When the Brooklyn boy visited Manhattan, he delighted in opera and the theater, particularly "all Shakspere's [*sic*] acting dramas, played wonderfully well."

Whitman's collection of poetry entitled *Leaves of Grass* is now recognized as America's cultural declaration of independence, and he is regarded as America's greatest poet and most original voice. It seems counterintuitive, even un-American, to think of him or his work as inspired by older European ideas of greatness. And yet the influence of Shakespeare stayed with him—not just for what the bard wrote but how he lived and worked. Preparing the first edition of *Leaves of Grass* in 1855, Whitman counted the number of words on a typical page of Shakespeare's writings and strove to make his own word counts match. Whitman also took notes on Shakespeare's biography, paying close attention to the parallels between them. He was intrigued that Shakespeare, like himself, was one of eight children, that he was a "handsome and well-shaped man," and that by age twenty-seven he "was already the father of three children—never seems to have amoured his wife afterward—nor did they live together." His notebooks include descriptions of Shakespeare—"bargained, was thrifty, borrowed money, loaned money had lawsuits"; "did right and wrong . . . committed follies, debaucheries, crimes"—that seem to be echoed by the confessional narrator of "Crossing Brooklyn Ferry," who "Blabbed, blushed, resented, lied, stole, grudged,/Had guile, anger, lust, hot wishes I dared not speak."

Whitman saw in Shakespeare a model for a literary life, for better and for worse. Even more unusually, the so-called father of free verse was impressed by Shakespeare's use of the sonnet's restrictive form. "For superb finish, style, beauty, I know of nothing in all literature to come up to these sonnets," he told his friend Horace Traubel. "They have been a great worry to the fellows, and to me too—a puzzle, the sonnets being of one character, the plays another." Though he owned few books, he possessed an 1847 copy of *The Poems of William Shakespeare* that included the entire sonnet sequence and "The Rape of Lucrece," prefaced with a passionate note from Shakespeare to the Earl of Southampton ("The love I dedicate to your Lordship is without end"). "Shakespeare wrote his 'sugar'd sonnets' early—probably soon after his appearance in London," Whitman noted, adding that "the beautiful young man so passionately treated, and so subtly the thread of the sonnets is without doubt *the Earl of Southampton.*" He was impressed that the Earl "made Shakespere [*sic*] the magnificent gift of a thousand pounds—Southampton was nine years the youngest—the ancient Greek friendship, seems to have existed between the two." Whitman's enduring interest in the culture of ancient Greece inspired his use of a time-honored code word for same-sex love.

Caught up in the craze for identifying the real person behind the "Fair Youth" of Shakespeare's sonnets, Whitman would surely understand our interest in finding him in his own writings. Is "Live Oak, with Moss" about Whitman's affectionate and erotic relationships with his own versions of the "Fair Youth"? Is the narrator Whitman himself, as Walt and so many others have speculated of Shakespeare in his sonnets? It is difficult to *not* imagine Whitman himself as the voice of these intimate, impassioned expressions of self, and his secrecy about the poems invites us to consider his motivations for being so guarded. The narrator is, after all, a man (IV's "brethren," VII's "his," and VIII's "other men" confirm it), a poet (II, V, VI, VII, XI) who, like Whitman, saw live oak trees in Louisiana (II). Yet it's always a tricky business to conflate the author with his characters. Attempting a pure autobiographical reading of "Live Oak, with Moss" is as futile as trying to pin down Shakespeare as the "I" of his sonnets. Each and all of these poems resist straightforward explications, defy our attempts to map out real relationships, and encourage ambiguity rather than resolution. Whitman seems to have followed Shakespeare's lead in making a "puzzle" of his poems.

Even if "Live Oak, with Moss" doesn't tell a factually accurate story, the subject of these poems was of such immense personal relevance to him that he wrote them in the first person and kept them to himself. Whether or not Whitman experienced a horrific breakup (the subject of VIII), a thrilling reunion (III), or a formidable crush (XI), he had such all-consuming thoughts, pictures, and aspirations about same-sex love that he put them on paper. Which leads us to a mysterious note he wrote on the verso of an early draft of "Live Oak, with Moss" II.

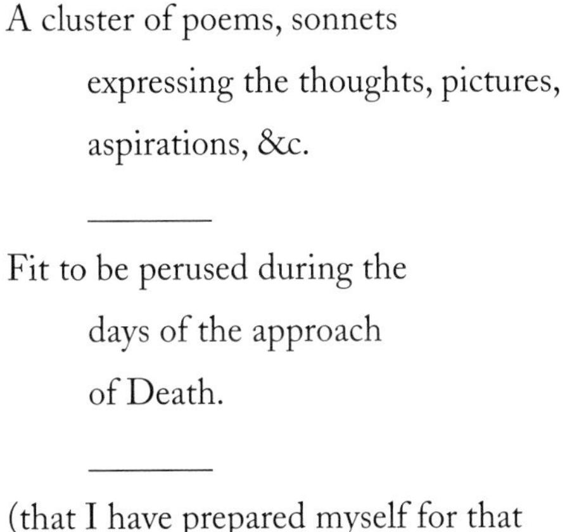

Poems

A cluster of poems, sonnets
expressing the thoughts, pictures,
aspirations, &c.

Fit to be perused during the
days of the approach
of Death.

(that I have prepared myself for that
purpose.—

(Remember now — — —
Remember then — — —

His plan is a poem of its own. Whitman indented its lines in the same way he formatted the other "Live Oak, with Moss" poems and may have even retitled it from "Poems" to "Poem." Apparently, he was struck with an idea for a poetic cluster around the same time he worked on a poem now known by its first line, "I saw in Louisiana a live-oak growing." Also on his mind was the idea of writing sonnets—indeed, the completed "Live Oak, with Moss" cluster resembles Shakespeare's "sugar'd sonnets" in both theme and form. Whitman's twelve, like Shakespeare's one hundred fifty-four, explore "ancient Greek friendship" through a nonlinear series of experiences and feelings, further complicated by multiple objects of love, lust and affection; both honor but also experiment with the sonnet's traditional fourteen lines of iambic pentameter. Even Whitman's use of Roman numerals as titles—an anomaly in his canon—may be borrowed from the headings for the sonnets in his copy of *The Poems of William Shakespeare*. On this single surviving page outlining a plan for what would become "Live Oak, with Moss," Whitman pondered a new type of poetry and a new relationship to his art.

Whitman was at work on his true "songs of myself." The "Poems" note hints that they didn't come easily: the open parentheses of the final cramped lines only appear in his private writings, where they indicate an uncomfortable or incomplete idea. Almost all pronouns are left out, as if Whitman is being furtive about whose thoughts he is expressing. The struggling poet planning "Live Oak, with Moss" seems more inwardly reflective than the all-embracing bard who declares "every atom belonging to me as good belongs to you" in the first poem of the first edition of *Leaves of Grass*.

Whitman indicates that "Live Oak, with Moss" is "fit to be perused" at a particular time, "during the days of the approach of Death." Death was a prominent theme from his first poems to his last, less as an end of physical existence or a close to a way of life and more of a welcome escape, even a beautiful thing. In an 1851 lecture to the Brooklyn Art Union, Whitman argued for a shift away from symbolizing Death as a "mouldering skull" to a "beautiful youth" reposing with his brother Sleep "in the arms of night." Perhaps the Death that he awaited while writing "Live Oak, with Moss" was a version of this beautiful youth, who would lead him from a life of suppressed desire to one of open affirmation and demonstration. And perhaps "Death" would enable him to express freely what he now kept to himself on these pages. "Remember now — — —/Remember then — — —" may thus be a memorandum to honor these unsettled, uncertain days of preparation when he was finally able to transcend them.

Did Whitman ever experience the new life he anticipated? In the first "Calamus" poem in *Leaves of Grass* (1860), he sings of a birth "this delicious Ninth Month, in my forty-first year" and proceeds "To tell the secret of my nights and days,/To celebrate the need of comrades." "Live Oak, with Moss" was the inner spark that ignited the open flames of the "Calamus" cluster. Yet after their publication, he never wrote such celebratory, erotically charged verse again. Though he republished "Calamus" in every subsequent edition of *Leaves of Grass*, the cluster decreased in size from forty-five in 1860 to thirty-nine in 1891–92. And the most complex, deeply intimate portraits in "Calamus" are poems originally included in the "Live Oak, with Moss" cluster (III, V, and VIII, later "Calamus" 3, 8, and 9—the first substantially revised over time, the latter two dropped after 1860). Adding to the growing silence was Whitman's lack of mention of his book of same-sex love poems. His reticence is made more poignant by the survival of his "Poems" plan, long after "Live Oak, with Moss" ceased to be.

Now, as Whitman's words encircle New York City's first AIDS Memorial, as modern-day sonnets confirm that "love is love is love is love is love is love is love is love," the "Death" that Whitman awaited has at last shown his beautiful face. As we jointly honor Whitman's two-hundredth birthday and the fiftieth anniversary of the Stonewall riots in 2019, the day has also come to peruse the "poems, sonnets expressing the thoughts, pictures, aspirations" of the first gay American of letters.

Let us remember then, as we will remember now.

Whitman assembled the "Live Oak, with Moss" book while living with his family at 91½ Classon Avenue, Brooklyn, between May 1856 and May 1859. With his father deceased, his youngest brother, Edward, unable to work, and alcoholism and mental illness affecting at least two other siblings, the household experienced constant money and personal troubles. Louisa Whitman rented rooms to help pay the bills; Walt and Eddy shared a bed in the third-floor attic. The house was far out from the center of Brooklyn and a six-mile round-trip from Manhattan's attractions—all in all, not an inspiring base for an aspiring poet.

Whitman had been disappointed by the reception and sales of his first two editions of *Leaves of Grass* (1855 and 1856), printed without publishers and financed by his own funds. Yet even in the chaotic Classon Avenue house, he busily planned for the next edition of the *Leaves*—his "New Bible" of American democracy—and wrote seventy poems in 1857 alone. He must have been encouraged by the pilgrimages of notable figures curious about the author of a book deemed "extraordinary" by America's first man of letters, Ralph Waldo Emerson. Renowned social reformer Bronson Alcott recorded his visit to the Whitman family home in November 1856 (published in *The Journals of Bronson Alcott*, 1938). Ascending the "narrow flights of stairs" to Walt's bedroom, he took note of "a Hercules, a Bacchus, and a satyr . . . pasted, unframed, upon the rude walls." More striking than his surroundings was the man himself:

> Broad-shouldered, rouge-fleshed, Bacchus-browed, bearded like a satyr, and rank, he wears his man-bloomer in defiance of everybody, having these as every thing else after his own fashion, and for example to all men hereafter. Red flannel undershirt, open-breasted, exposing his brawny neck; striped calico jacket over this, the collar Byroneal, with coarse cloth overalls buttoned to it; cowhide boots; a heavy round-about, with huge outside pockets and buttons to match, and a slouched hat, for house and street alike. Eyes gray, unimaginative, cautious yet sagacious; his voice deep, sharp, tender sometimes and almost melting. When talking will recline upon the couch at length, pillowing his head upon his bended arm, and informing you naively how lazy he is, and slow.

Alcott found it irresistible to read meaning into Whitman's distinct physical appearance. The poet seemed to be the very embodiment of his poems: raw, sensual, luxuriant, democratic, original. Sporting billowy trousers that resembled bloomers (America's first pants for women, introduced by female activists in 1851), Whitman showed his allegiance to the fledgling women's rights movement by cross-dressing. His predilection for looser, ready-to-wear items such as roundabouts or sack coats over the tighter-fitting frock coats and tailored jackets favored in his day foreshadowed the establishment of today's American uniform: casual clothing as free and easygoing as the country aims to be. The relaxed presentation of his body, the slowness of his movements, the deep but nonintellectual gaze all seem to be physical manifestations of his thoughts, or what Whitman described as the soul.

The world has always loved looking at Walt Whitman, and Whitman made it easy to do so. As the most photographed American poet of the nineteenth century, Whitman is also one of the most recognizable of literary figures. Descriptions of his physique (including his height and weight), face, affect, and bearing abound in his writings. His lifelong curation of his self-image may have been inspired by phrenology, a popular pseudoscience that took hold of his imagination in the 1840s. "Bumpology" held that mental and emotional faculties are indicated by the skull's conformation; a skilled phrenologist can read character by recording the position and size of bumps on the head. At first skeptical, Whitman became increasingly fascinated with the pseudoscience as well as its New York practitioners Orson and Lorenzo Fowler and Samuel Wells. The team maintained The Phrenological Cabinet in Manhattan's Newspaper Row district, where Whitman had his bumps read in 1849.

Whitman considered his phrenological reading a prime indicator of his literary promise: according to Orson Fowler, nature had chosen him for the profession of poet. He proudly published his chart in *Leaves of Grass*, along with Fowler's "Phrenological Notes," and the first of his so-called "leading traits" became foundational to his developing ideas of sexuality and identity. *Friendship* or *adhesiveness*, pseudoscientifically speaking, referred to any propensity for strong emotional attachments with someone of the same sex. But Whitman knew from his readings on Greek culture that *friendship* could accommodate a particular "Domestic Propensity" not listed in Fowler and Wells' guidebooks. Before Karl-Maria Kertbeny's first booklet on gay rights was published in 1869 and the clinical term *homosexual* was first used in English (in

Charles Gilbert Chaddock's 1892 translation of Richard von Krafft-Ebing's *Psychopathia Sexualis*), Whitman worked to create a language for what he was and felt. His predilection for phrenological terminology, from *friendship* (with its convenient associations to Greek same-sex love) in "Live Oak, with Moss" to *adhesiveness* introduced in the "Calamus" poems of *Leaves of Grass* (1860), is a reminder that he regarded sexual identity as a natural part of the body, like the curves of the skull. He was a proponent of the belief—new to his day—that it wasn't just performed or expressed but integral to one's being.

THE RIPENING

In the 1850s Whitman began seeking adhesiveness on the streets of New York. The bigness, loneliness, and romantic potential of his Mannahatta is captured by Victor Prevost, whose photographs bring a historical dimension to the vision of New York in this book. Arriving from Paris in 1848, Prevost quickly fell in love with the cityscape. While most photographers of his time succumbed to the fad of taking portrait daguerreotypes, he searched for inanimate subjects for his calotypes, large and detailed waxed paper negatives. Just as Whitman was writing the first love poems to the city, Prevost was celebrating it through the first extensive photo series of its vistas and buildings. Images of the Old Herring's Safe Factory on Manhattan's West Side (circa 1854), P. Gori's Marble Working Establishment on Broadway and Twentieth Street (1853), and Jeremiah Gurney's Daguerrean Gallery at Broadway and Leonard (1855) retain a haunting quality because of the long exposure time required to produce early photographs. Though New Yorkers didn't stay still long enough to be captured by Prevost's lens, the buildings he photographed have their own discernible character. Their facades can be read like human faces, hinting at the complicated stories that played out behind their closed doors.

Whitman, like Prevost, found New York City an inspiring place to explore—and to explore himself. The notebooks he toted on his walks include lists of men's names, ages, addresses, and physical descriptions:

> Tom Riley (handsome Irish fighter
> John Kiernan (loafer, young saucy looking pretty goodlooking
> Dave (rich, (white hat.) rides on Broadway
> Jack (big young fellow sits corner Adams & Myrtle live 4th Ave
> Arthur, big round sandy hair coarse, open
> Peleg, round head & face young
> Wallace, (sailor boy English was in Japan)
> John Stoothoof, (police South ferry smallish sized)
> Peter Dempster (Cor Kent & Myrtle open faced—gay)

Line after line of such details comprise what might be considered Whitman's longest, gayest poems. Utilizing the open parentheses seen in the "Poems" note throughout, such as for "Bob—(hermaphrodite", he sometimes interjected personal comments: "went in Castle Garden with me"; "slept with him." Other contemporaneous writings also make use of suggestive confessional language, such as an unpublished manuscript poem announcing that its author is "full of wickedness" and recalls "many a smutch'd deed." These alleged acts remain off Whitman's pages, though observers have left tantalizing clues. On March 17, 1860, the comic journal *Vanity Fair* published "Counter-Jumps. A Poemettina. After Walt Whitman," written from the perspective of a counter jumper or shop assistant—an occupation considered unmanly during Whitman's day. "I am the creature of weak depravities;/I am the Counter-jumper;/I sound my feeble yelp over the woofs of the World," sings the diminutive dandy in the accompanying sketch, while a giant, suave Whitman attempts to capture him with his oversized hat. The title is as parodic as the poem: it is Whitman who is "after" the counter jumper.

The creators of the poem and sketch—and, no doubt, various models for the counter jumper—were Whitman's drinking companions at Pfaff's beer cellar, an underground bar and the birthplace of American bohemia. The building still stands at 647 Broadway, just north of Bleecker Street in Greenwich Village. During Whitman's day, Pfaff's was located in the theater district and thus attracted performers and journalists as well as a workmanly crowd. While the proprietor Charles Pfaff served hearty German fare and fresh lager, its impresario Henry Clapp held court at a special table under the vaulted sidewalk. The lively gatherings of the era's most progressive intellectuals and superstars, such as the cross-dressing performer Adah Isaacs Menken and actress Ada Clare (an unwed mother who preached the doctrine of free love); the intimate friendship between members of the Fred Gray Association, perhaps the country's first gay club; the long, low hall of tables filled with smoke and city workers: all of this proved irresistible to Walt. Though he never had or would ever again be a regular anywhere, he claimed he frequented Pfaff's "almost every night" during the late '50s and early '60s, just as he was working on "Live Oak, with Moss" and completing the third edition of the *Leaves*.

One of the men Whitman met at Pfaff's was Fred Vaughan, a stagecoach driver of Irish descent about twenty years his junior (and a type Whitman favored: Peter Doyle, the great, later love of his life, was a Limerick-born horsecar conductor twenty-four years younger than he). Vaughan may have been Whitman's first boyfriend, and their correspondence indicates that they lived together for a while on Classon Avenue. They seem to have shared a passionate attachment, and yet there are signs that something was not quite right. In a letter dated March 27, 1860, Vaughan reviewed a lecture he had heard on male friendship. "What do you think of them setting you and myself and one or two others we know up in some public place with an immense placard on our breasts reading Sincere Freinds!!! [*sic*] Good doctrine that but I think the theory preferable to the practice." Was Fred perhaps uncomfortable about public displays of affection? Walt, on the other hand, may have been more eager. Wrestling with his feelings for Pete in 1870, he wrote in a notebook: "Depress the adhesive nature/It is in excess—making life a torment . . . Remember Fred Vaughan."

Still, it's unlikely that Vaughan served as sole inspiration for "Live Oak, with Moss." Their relationship only began in 1859, as Whitman was inscribing final drafts of the poems into his notebook. It's also difficult to believe that they were exclusively dedicated to each other. The Fred Gray Association, the confessional poem drafts, the counter jumpers, his jam-packed little black books—such factors indicate that Whitman's newly awakened adhesive nature was not so easily depressed. Physically, emotionally, and artistically, Whitman was experimenting while working on "Live Oak, with Moss."

THE ROOTS

Emboldened by the company he kept at what may have been America's first gay bar, liberated by his fellow Pfaffians' acceptance of free love and free verse, Whitman wrote his most intimate expressions of self during the years he frequented the bohemian enclave. But the roots of "Live Oak, with Moss" run deeper. The poems in the book are too neatly written to be Whitman's first drafts. Earlier versions of two of them do in fact exist: predecessors to II and III are housed in the New York Public Library's Berg Collection and the University of Virginia's Albert and Shirley Small Special Collections Library, respectively. Though these manuscripts cannot be dated, a sexualized reference to "branches of liveoak [*sic*]" in the first edition of *Leaves of Grass* indicate that Whitman was utilizing this symbol before the book's publication in June 1855.

Another clue to the origins of "Live Oak, with Moss" exists on a palimpsest. Written in pencil and then erased on notebook leaf 13, under the second line of "Live Oak, with Moss" VIII, is the note "finished in the other city." Since the ink in which VIII is written is unmarked by the erasure, it is probable that "finished in the other city" was written earlier than the poem, and then erased. Of course, the note may be disconnected from the "Live Oak, with Moss" poems. But it also may be a reference to New Orleans, the only "other city" that played a significant role in his life before the Civil War, and the only city in which he saw the live oak trees that inspired the title and symbolic image of the cluster.

It is unlikely that Whitman would have denigrated either Manhattan or Brooklyn—the cities that dominated his existence through his first four decades—as "the other." But the New Orleans he explored from February through May 1848 was certainly another world. After being fired from the *Brooklyn Daily Eagle*, Walt made his first venture beyond New York and outside his family's radius of influence. No one knew him, and he knew nobody except his favorite sibling Thomas Jefferson, who accompanied him on this trip and also tagged along on Walt's visits to Pfaff's ten years later. In an article entitled "New Orleans in 1848," Whitman describes his fondness for the "old French Market," the "crowded and bustling levees" and the "splendid and roomy and leisurely bar-rooms." He publicly defended risqué theatrical shows such as Dr. Colyer's troupe of "Model Artists," wrote character sketches of questionable "ladies" such as "Miss Dusky Grisette," and took pleasure finding "a real rough diamond among my chance encounters." He also had his first photograph taken: looking out from the shiny surface of this daguerreotype is an insouciant dandy, sleepy-eyed with arm perched precariously on a cane—sexy and self-conscious at once.

One of the great mysteries of American literary history is how Walter Whitman Jr.—the insecure flaneur captured in this image, intriguing yet conventional in clothing and affect—became the radiant, charismatic everyman who fixes his gaze on the readers of *Leaves of Grass* from its frontispiece. It's tempting to speculate that a sexual awakening in this permissive, faraway place inspired the sea change in his personal and his literary style from 1848 to 1855. Whitman himself provoked such theories in 1890 when, pressured by John Addington Symonds to discuss the sexuality of the "Calamus" poems, he claimed that "I have had six children—two are dead—One living southern grandchild, fine boy, who writes to me occasionally." The first major biography of Whitman after his death—Henry Bryan Binns' *A Life of Walt Whitman* (1905)—proposed that Whitman had indeed had an affair with a Southern woman during his New Orleans sojourn. The story was never substantiated and yet has had its defenders, probably inspired by the same homophobia that stifled "Live Oak, with Moss" for more than one hundred sixty years. Complicating this theory was scholar Emory Holloway's discovery of a manuscript draft of "Once I Pass'd Through a Populous City." The poem, ostensibly about New Orleans, originally focused on the narrator's encounter with a man (not a woman, as in its published version).

We may never discover what happened to Whitman in New Orleans, but we do know that he came away from that experience with one of the most potent symbols in all his writing. Though the Mid-Atlantic states in which Whitman spent his life have no equivalent to the live oak, he would have seen these giant trees daily in New Orleans. Letters written by Jeff to their mother describe their walks "every night" in a "very fine public park"—most probably Lafayette Square, just down St. Charles Avenue from his boardinghouse and his office at the *New Orleans Daily Crescent*. Now as then, visitors marvel at the sprawling limbs and ample shade of the live oaks lining the park's walkways. Walt's extended perambulations may have brought him to Audubon Park, home of one of the world's most famous live oaks, the eight-hundred-year-old Tree of Life, standing today with a thirty-five-foot girth and a crown of one hundred sixty-five feet.

It's easy to recognize the live oak as a symbol for Whitman in its grand size and stature and its "uttering [of] joyous leaves." But poem II invites us to look more closely. Whitman sees himself in its "rude, unbending, lusty" appearance: the muscular anthropomorphism of the thick limbs conveyed a primitive power and sensuality that he wanted associated with himself. Despite the erotic appeal of its stiff glistening leaves, deeply curving branches, and the luxuriant Spanish moss draping upon them, the tree stands "solitary in a wide flat space." The limb spread and luxurious canopy of the live oak prevent the growth of other trees and plants underneath it. Whitman marvels at the tree's singularity—perceives, perhaps, its likeness to his independent character and favored position as observer—but refuses to sympathize: "I wondered how it could utter joyous leaves, standing alone there without its friend, its lover near—for I knew I could not . . . " More difficult to conjecture is how a "twig with a certain number of leaves upon it" twined around with moss came to represent Whitman's idea of manly love—though the appearance of "branches of liveoak [*sic*]" in a catalogue of "the spread of my body" in "Song of Myself" (1855) suggests that they, along with "fibre of manly wheat" and a "nest of guarded duplicate eggs," serve as natural metaphors for male genitalia.

When Whitman decided to go public with these twelve poems—to tear them out of his notebook, edit and include them in the "Calamus" cluster of *Leaves of Grass* (1860)—he also renamed them using a more universal and recognizable symbol. The Southern live oaks Whitman saw in

Louisiana have a limited range in the Southeastern United States; *acorus calamus* (or sweet flag) is found on three continents as well as the wetlands of Brooklyn and Long Island (in fact, a Calamus Avenue runs a few miles from Whitman's Classon Avenue home). Live oaks stand alone; calamus proliferates and grows together in colonies. Whereas the meaning of the live oak was personal and particular to Whitman, readers of the "Calamus" cluster need only see an image of the plant to comprehend his subject: calamus is overtly phallic, with a solid, cylindrical spadix emerging from its leaves. The title fearlessly sets forth its focus on male sexuality, even while it possesses the broad, democratic accessibility of the title *Leaves of Grass*.

THE REASON

As the poems' deeper purpose and meanings probably eluded Whitman himself, they will certainly escape us. And yet scholars have attempted to identify a story in "Live Oak, with Moss" since Bowers discovered the manuscripts. "The poems appear to be highly unified and to make up an artistically complete story of attachment, crisis, and renunciation," he asserted; about forty years later, Alan Helms agreed that "the love narrative of 'Live Oak' tells a fairly simple story of infatuation, abandonment, and accommodation." Hershel Parker, who took issue with other aspects of Helms's interpretation, concurred that "the sequence traces the course of a man's love for another man, their happiness together, and the aftermath of their relationship, which proves to be only a love affair, not the lifelong union the speaker had hoped for."

In her 2011 study of the poems, Betsy Erkkila introduced a departure from this line of thought, noting that "the story Whitman tells in 'Live Oak, with Moss' may not be simple, single, or self-coherent." Indeed, to suggest that the poems tell the story of a "man's love for another man" is to overlook the fact that "Live Oak, with Moss" references "lovers" and "friends" in nearly as many poems as "lover" and "friend." Why presume these poems focus on a couple, when exclusive relationships are found in only seven of the twelve poems and though Whitman was probably not monogamous while writing them? If Whitman was reading Shakespeare's sonnets while working on his own, he would have encountered myriads of sexual possibilities including polyamory, omnisexuality, and open relationships. Furthermore, to assume that Whitman wrote "Live Oak, with Moss" as a linear narrative sequence is to forget his nonlinear, nontraditional approach to his life and art. Whitman very seldom wrote story-poems, and none of his other poetry clusters present a coherent narrative. There is evidence, too, that Whitman experimented with the order of the twelve poems before or while transcribing them: a draft predating "Live Oak, with Moss" III labels that poem IV, and a crossed-out IX is clearly visible at the top of the manuscript of "Live Oak, with Moss" VIII.

Whitman's creation of the term *cluster* for his "sonnets," and favoring that over the more common *sequence*, is another sign of his attempt to break from convention. A *cluster* is an organic grouping, more associated with acorns or stars than poems. It's also a term that winks toward the testicles, like the "life-swelling yolks" of "The Sleepers" or the "ripened long-round walnuts" of "Spontaneous Me." Whitman's "Live Oak, with Moss" can be considered a natural cluster because of its dominant imagery: air, water, fire, and earth. What is natural and elemental by association is Whitman's theme—sex and intimacy, particularly manly love. Same-sex passion is not a "gross obscenity," as Rufus Griswold declared *Leaves of Grass* was in an 1855 review (it was his duty, he wrote, to identify its vileness: "*Peccatum illud horribile, inter Christianos non nominandum*," Latin for "that horrible crime not to be named among Christians" and a long-lasting expression of homophobia). Expressing desire isn't dirty or profane (a *New York Daily Times* reviewer declared the second edition of the *Leaves* a "mucked abomination" and Whitman "like the priests of Belus . . . he wreathes around his brow the emblems of the phallic worship"). Descriptions of the body could be more than the pornography "sought out and laughed over by lewd women and prurient boys and hoary-headed old lechers," as the *Springfield Daily Republican* commented on *Leaves of Grass* (1860).

"Live Oak, with Moss" doesn't *declare* manly love organic, natural, and pure; it takes as a given that it *is*. And it is, whether it's expressed between two men or several men or even by one person fantasizing about a future love. You might "seek [your] life-long lover" (I) one day, and "think of little else than [my friends]" (II) the next. Love can be "tender" (VII) or "fierce and terrible" (XI)—or both, and more. The friend you love "may lay sleeping by [your] side" (III); or there may be "other men, in other lands" whom you wish to love (IV). Love may be public and demonstrative, like the "two men I saw to-day on the pier" (VI); or secret, a "subtle electric fire that for your sake is burning within me" (X).

"Live Oak, with Moss" is Whitman's first sustained attempt to address the naturalness of love beyond traditional heteronormative boundaries. Parts of the twelve poems of the first edition of the *Leaves* allude to manly love, but this theme is central to all twelve in the cluster. Whitman may have envisioned "Live Oak, with Moss" as a compact, intimate version of *Leaves of Grass*—a move from broad democratic spaces to private interiors. If *Leaves of Grass* provides a grand calendar of poems teaching us what it means to be American, the twelve "Live Oak, with Moss" poems can each be absorbed twice a day, in sleeping and waking hours, as we dream and demonstrate how we too can express ourselves openly and authentically.

LIVE OAK LEAVES

Passionately searching, pensive and questioning, blissfully happy, yearning, resolved and committed, sympathetic, reminiscent, downtrodden and desperate, hopeful, secretly aroused, uncontrollably lustful, seeking and challenging: these poems are moving pictures of manly love in its many moods. They do not and could not tell a simple, linear story of an affair. Instead the poems remind us of nature's cycles and regenerative power. Love is desired, is sometimes even won, can be lost; even so, love returns. The "flames of me" in poem I may appear doused in VIII but become "fierce and terrible" by XI. The sea waves of poem I will continue to rush in and out. The full moon of III will return. And XII's hot red blood of friendship unceasingly circulates, despite the forces that have tried to stop it through time.

There is no single starting point in a natural cluster. But a Whitmanic place to begin is at its most self-revelatory moment—which is also the cluster's darkest. "Live Oak, with Moss" VIII became "Calamus" 9 in *Leaves of Grass* (1860), but it was one of the few poems in Whitman's canon (with "Live Oak, with Moss" V, which became "Calamus" 8 in 1860) that never appeared in the *Leaves* again after its first publication. "Calamus" 8 and 9 may be unknown even to avid Whitman readers because modern editions of his poetry usually reprint the text of *Leaves of Grass* (1891–92), which excludes both works.

But those familiar with Shakespeare may recognize the provocative subjects and experimental style of his sonnets in Whitman's own. Scholars have claimed that Whitman deliberately modeled poem VIII on specific Shakespearean sonnets such as CXXI and XXIX, both dedicated to the Fair Youth. Like a sonnet, poem VIII has a turn or *volta* indicating a change in direction in its argument: after line six, Whitman shifts from statements beginning with the long, drawn-out sound of "hours" (a mournful reminder of what was "ours") to a flood of anxious questions. Critically, it is missing two of the sonnet's traditional fourteen lines; but even this might indicate Shakespeare's role in shaping "Live Oak, with Moss." While the final couplet in Shakespeare's sonnets often helps bring closure to the preceding lines, the possibly deliberate lack of this device emphasizes VIII's unresolved ending. The missing couplet of Whitman's sonnet VIII is a reminder of the missing couple.

Shakespeare would have approved of Whitman's reshaping of the conventional sonnet form; he did so himself. He, too, wrote a twelve-line sonnet—CXXVI—the last in the sequence dedicated to the Fair Youth, and a farewell to "my young boy" who only temporarily has power to "hold Time's fickle glass, his sickle hour." While the hours pass all too swiftly for Shakespeare's love, they drag on—and on—for Whitman's speaker. The narrator can't seem to escape his thoughts, whether he is literally running from them (as he does in the first half) or wrestling with difficult questions in the last six lines. His words don't seem to move on but instead mirror each other, most strikingly in the last line: "Does he see himself reflected in me? In these hours does he see the face of his hours reflected?" Indeed, *reflective* may be the word that best characterizes VIII's content and style.

The subject of all these reflections is a statement at the heart of the poem, embraced by parentheses: "I am ashamed—but it is useless—I am what I am." The poet of "Live Oak, with Moss" has come out. His immediate feelings are shame and helplessness, and the latter half of the poem is spent seeking company in his misery. "Is there even one other like me," he asks, and his flood of anxious questions suggests his anticipation of the isolation that his declaration may bring on. As resigned as he may seem, he has delivered a courageous statement of identification and affirmation: "I am what I am." And though he is unable to find sympathy or companionship, he offers himself as someone to see ourselves in—someone to reflect upon—in our own hours of need.

If VIII is the deepest, poem III is the happiest. It is the other twelve-line sonnet in this cluster, and like VIII, III has a *volta* in the middle dividing the setup of "when"s from the response ("then I was happy"). Instead of presenting a series of slowly cycling reflections as in VIII, poem III continues to move forward toward a goal—a climax, in fact. Anticipating the coming of his lover, "each breath tasted sweeter," "my food nourished me more," and the "happy waters" rose until "I heard you beating the shores." The descriptions crescendo until the lovers lie side by side, faces turned toward each other, one arm over the other's chest. The image of two loving bodies so contentedly enwrapped, illuminated by the full moon, is the most serene and tender image in the cluster and perhaps in all of Whitman's poetry.

But Whitman labored over this portrayal of bliss. The flap pasted over the last four lines is an anomaly in "Live Oak, with Moss" and shows his significant dissatisfaction with the poem's original ending. III was also one of the cluster's most heavily edited poems after Whitman tore it out of the book to revise it as "Calamus" 11. What remained consistent from the poem's first appearance to its final state in *Leaves of Grass* (1891–92) are the framing images of the Capitol building and the full moon shining on the lovers, symbols of two very different kinds of success. Can one have both? "Live Oak, with Moss" III suggests that one might not be able to balance or even want a sense of fulfillment both at work and at home. The speaker clearly does not find happiness being "praised in the Capitol" but in the coming and the touch of his lover.

In "Live Oak, with Moss" II, he is less sure-footed about his valuation of private over public, social life over writing life—though he also hints at personal sacrifices that may accompany an ambitious, civic-minded career. The narrator marvels at the productiveness of the solitary live oak "uttering joyous leaves" while "standing there alone without its friend, its lover." He claims that he could not do the same—twice—as if needing to convince himself of this statement. After all, he has already admitted that the tree "made me think of myself." Deciding to answer to the pressing urges of manly love rather than to stay true to his poetic vision was clearly more difficult than he admits, or this poem would not exist.

The narrator's obsessive thoughts about his friends make poem II sound as if it were written early during his explorations of manly love. By poem V, he has found someone for whom he will sacrifice his art; but he has again "taken my pen to record" in VI, and in VII acknowledges that he will leave a literary legacy (though he asks to be remembered for the "measureless ocean of love within him," not his poems). The closest to a sequence within "Live Oak, with Moss," these four poems narrate the poet's wrestle with his two great passions. In V the poet recounts the four-step process that shaped him as the New World's "singer of songs." But writing such poems no longer brings him joy; instead, "I am to go with him I love, and he is to go with me,/It is to be enough for each of us that we are together—We never separate again." Apparently, America had not provided him with the loving response he had hoped for; even now, he addresses the landscape as "you," and as if it were capable of answering him. In the big picture, however, he may have expected too much from all of his potential partners, including the "perfect love" of poem V. There is no sign of his supposedly ultra-attentive friend in the following poem or anywhere else in "Live Oak, with Moss." The narrator of poem VI is not a participant but an observer, recording a scene between lovers instead of playing a part.

Much remains unknown about our guide, though this is clear: he writes poems convincing himself to stop writing, but he doesn't have to convince himself to start up again. He just does. As ready as he is to relinquish all for a passion-filled life, writing proves too irresistible, too instinctive. He has also realized that he can combine his interests by singing songs of manly love—different "New World songs" than he claimed to sing in V.

In VII, the poet speaks to the future and demands "bards of ages hence" know "who I was underneath that impassive exterior." The many claims he makes of his actions and feelings might be just that, here and in X and XI; all three poems seem to describe the suppression of gay longings behind a straight face. But the poems can also be read as attempts to remove conventional masks. The narrator of VII admits that he becomes physically ill ("O sick! sick!") at the thought of his lover losing interest in him. Poems X and XI go even deeper, and attempt to describe the very spark and igniting of sexual desire. In "Live Oak, with Moss" X, our guide equates his burning passion with a "subtle electric fire" that can't be seen or felt by its target. In XI, earth is his "likeness" and his libido is compared to an earthquake in its magnitude and force. The carnality of his longings is emphasized by his choice of an athlete—for Whitman, a classical ideal physique—for a lover. Lust is elemental in these descriptions, as real and as powerful as nature itself. Though he writes that he "dare not tell it in words," he has found a way to communicate the intensity of incommunicable feelings.

The cluster begins with another poem equating physical desire with the elements. The negatives in poem I actually serve an affirmative purpose: his passion is hungrier, more constant and generously spread forth than fire, water, air, or living earthly things. The poem's imagery and even particular phrases echo "Bunch Poem" (later retitled "Spontaneous Me") from *Leaves of Grass* (1856), in which the narrator describes the "bunch" (i.e., his semen) "plucked at random from myself . . . I toss it carelessly to fall where it may." In "Live Oak, with Moss" I, his soul is likened to "down-balls of myriads of seeds . . . sailing gracefully, to drop where they may" as well as "perfumes" and "high rain-emitting clouds . . . borne through the open air, wafted in all directions, for friendship, for love." This playful portrayal of masturbation is a reminder that nineteenth century America classified homosexuality as a form of onanism, sex without a procreative function. For Whitman, "unnatural acts" such as autoeroticism and homoeroticism are at least as powerful as nature's own life-giving forces.

Poems IX, IV, and XII reach beyond immediate sensory pleasure to the emotional and psychological need for community and public acknowledgment. In IX, the poet introduces his boldest term for the "love of friends": manly love. By using this adjective, he attempts to overturn the nineteenth century's association of homosexuality with unmanliness (meaning effeminacy, weakness, or disgrace). The men of IX are "tender" but also "robust"; their affection is uninhibited and ineluctable—a "dream in a dream." Poem IV presents another vision of a "wise, beautiful, benevolent" community of men loving men. Though they are physically and culturally removed from each other, they are united in their "yearning" for brotherhood. Poem XII confirms that the bond between such men is biological and even detectable by each other. They share the "blood of friendship, hot and red" and "silently select" their companions.

"Live Oak, with Moss" begins and ends with the narrator seeking love, but he who initiated his search in unrestrained eagerness has become the master in poem XII. The poem's reference to friendship in this context recalls the ancient Greek friendship Whitman identified between Shakespeare and the Earl of Southampton and celebrated in "Pictures," a poem he had planned but failed to publish in 1860. Transporting the reader to Athens, Whitman describes how "couples or trios, young and old, clear-faced, and of perfect physique, walk with twined arms, in divine friendship, happy/Till, beyond, the master appears advancing—his form shows above the crowd, a head taller than they." The narrator of XII may enjoy an elevated position, but Whitman's choice of the French word *eleve* suggests that his student, too, will rise. Further, it directs attention back to the only place where Whitman heard French regularly spoken: New Orleans, the possible birthplace of his concept of manly love.

LIVE OAK LIVES ON

In early 1859 Whitman gathered eleven sheets of paper, folding them in halves and stitching them together along the fold to make a book of twenty-two leaves. He used this book (measuring about nine and a half by fifteen centimeters) to inscribe a series of twelve poems that he had been working on for some time. The first page is missing, though the cluster commences on the second leaf. The poems were written on the rectos of sheets two through eighteen, headed by Roman numerals.

Later that year, he tore out the leaves and cut and pasted together some parts of poems that had originally appeared on multiple sheets. He started testing various arrangements of the poems and integrating others into what would become the "Calamus" cluster of *Leaves of Grass* (1860). A thread still hanging from poem VII and pin punctures that match up through different sheets indicates that he tried to sew or pin together groupings. The pinholes are numerous—poems X and XI each have eighteen—so he must have put them together and taken them apart many times. He also pinned leaves together near their middles: a pin's entry and exit can be seen on the first sheet of VIII from the last "e" in "unfrequented" to the comma after "myself." Whitman employed this practice in his scrapbooks, which he sometimes enlivened with pressed leaves. Might the green spot on the "m" of "Calamus" at the top of poem I be a remnant of organic matter—a leaf of live oak or calamus—once pinned there? Are the pinkish stains on other pages also plant residue? Or blood? Noteworthy markings include the pink-rimmed pinhole interrupting "I dare not" and "tell" in XI and the brownish-pink fingerprint swooping over "me" on the second leaf of VIII—the actual hand of the poet and perhaps the hot red "blood of friendship" itself.

In addition to breaking up and rearranging "Live Oak, with Moss," Whitman edited the poems, modifying his original black ink drafts with pencil and a lighter ink. These revisions were not always for the better, sometimes sacrificing the earnestness of first inspiration for clarity or a more reserved tone. For example, in the original version of the last four lines of poem III (now hidden under a flap), the narrator hears the waters "beating" the shores, which connects with his heart "beating happier" because "he I love was returned and sleeping by my side." In Whitman's later revision, the waters "roll slowly continually" and their "hissing rustle" congratulates him, "For the friend I love lay sleeping by my side." The poem's original joy and urgency has been replaced by a more controlled, perhaps more ominous mood. This change in tone is also felt in his update to the last line of IV: "O I know we should be brethren—I know I should be happy with them" becomes "O I think we should be brethren—I think I should be happy with them" in Whitman's later edit, a newly cautious comment regarding "other men in other lands."

This edition thus follows the lead of scholar Steven Olsen-Smith in providing Whitman's final articulation of the "Live Oak, with Moss" cluster, just before he took the notebook apart and started rethinking his project. Olsen-Smith's 2012 study of the poems reveals that there were multiple stages of revisions to the manuscripts after disassembly, yet Bowers and the subsequent editors of "Live Oak, with Moss" included these later edits in their transcriptions of the poems. Olsen-Smith is the first to attempt to restore Whitman's ultimate vision of "Live Oak, with Moss," so his text—like this one—differs subtly and sometimes significantly from every other edition. The intention is to bring the reader inside "Live Oak, with Moss" in its most stable, intact, original form.

You now hold in hand twelve of the most personally meaningful poems that Walt Whitman ever wrote. Though the poems as you encounter them were seen previously by his eyes alone, their undeniable power to live beyond their moment—to touch other lives—has inspired this book.

The songs left to be sung, as Whitman would say, are your own.

—Karen Karbiener

THE NOTEBOOK

#14 Calamus-~~Leaves~~.
p.360 ~~Live Oak, with Moss.~~

II.

Not the heat flames up and consumes,
Not the sea-waves hurry in and out,
Not the air, delicious and dry, the air of the ripe summer, bears lightly along white down-balls of myriads of seeds, wafted, sailing gracefully, to drop where they may,
Not these – O none of these, more than the flames of me, consuming, burning for his love whom I love – O none, more than I hurrying in and out;
Does the tide hurry, seeking something, and never give up? – O I, the same, to seek my life-long lover;
O nor down-balls nor perfumes, nor the high rain-emitting clouds, are borne through the open air, more than my copious soul is borne through the open air, wafted in all directions, for friendship, for love. –

Calamus 20
p 364

II

I saw in Louisiana a
live-oak growing,
All alone stood it, and the
moss hung down from the
branches,
Without any companion it grew
there, glistening out with
joyous leaves of dark green,
And its look, rude, unbending,
lusty, made me think of
myself;
But I wondered how it could
utter joyous leaves, standing
alone there without its friend,
its lover – For I knew I could
not;
And I plucked a twig with
a certain number of leaves
upon it, and twined around
it a little moss, and brought
it away – And I have placed
it in sight in my room,

It is. not needed to remind
me as of my friends, (for I
believe lately I think of little
else than of them,)
Yet it remains to me a
curious token — it makes me think of manly love; ~~I write~~
~~these pieces, and name~~
~~them after~~ it ;
For all that, and though the
~~tree~~ live oak glistens there in Louis-
iana, solitary in a wide
flat space, uttering joyous
leaves all its life, without
a friend, a lover, near — I
know very well I could
not.

(18—357)

II II II

When I heard at the close of
the day how I had been
praised in the Capitol, still
it was not a happy night
for me that followed;
Nor
~~And else~~, when I caroused — Or
— Nor favorite
when my plans were accom-
was I really happy
plished — ~~it was well enough~~ —
~~Still I was not happy;~~
the that.
But ~~that~~ day when ~~when~~ I rose
at dawn from the bed of
perfect health, electric, in-
haling sweet breath,
When I saw the full moon
in the west grow pale and
disappear in the morning light,
When I wandered alone over the
beach and undressing, bathed,
laughing with the waters, and
saw the sun rise,

4

And when I thought how
my friend, my lover, was
coming, then O I was happy;
O ~~then~~ each breath tasted
sweeter — and all that day my
food nourished me more — And
the beautiful day passed well,
And the next came with equal
joy — And with the next, at
evening, came my friend,
And that night, O you happy
waters, I heard you beating
the shores — But my heart
beat happier than you — for
he I love was returned and
sleeping by my side,
And that night in the stillness
his face was inclined towards
me, while the moon's clear
beams shone,
And his arm lay lightly over my
breast — And that night I
was happy.

Calamus 23

p. 367

V.

This moment as I sit alone, yearning and pensive, it seems to me there are other men, in other lands, yearning and pensive.

It seems to me I can look over and behold them, in Germany, France, Spain—Or far away in China, ~~or in~~ India, or Russia—talking other dialects

And it seems to me if I could know those men ~~better~~ I should love them as I love men in my own lands,

It seems to me they are as wise, beautiful, benevolent, as any in my own lands;

O I ~~know~~ think we should be brethren—I ~~know~~ think I should be happy with them.

6

Pamphlet 354
8

V.

Long I thought that knowledge alone would suffice me — O if I could but obtain knowledge!
Then ~~my lands~~ the Land of the Prairies — the south savannas engrossed me — me
For them I would live — I would be their orator;
Then I met the examples of old and new heroes — I heard ~~the examples~~ of warriors, sailors, and all dauntless persons —
And it seemed to me I too had it in me to be as dauntless as any, and would be so;
And then to finish all, it came to me to strike up the songs of the New World — And then I believed my life must be spent in singing;
But now take notice, Land of the prairies, Land of the south savannas, Ohio's land,

Take notice, you Kanuck woods
— and you, Lake Huron — and
all that with you roll toward
Niagara — and you Niagara
also,
And you, Californian mountains —
that you all find some one else
that he be your singer of songs,
For I can be your singer of songs
no longer — ~~I have passed ahead~~ —
I have ceased to enjoy them,
I have found him who loves me,
as I him, in perfect love,
With the rest I dispense — I sever
from all that I thought would
suffice me, for it does not — it
is now empty and tasteless
to me,
I heed knowledge, and the grandeur
of The States, and the examples
of heroes, no more,

8

I am indifferent to my own
songs – I am to go with
him I love, and he is to
go with me,
It is to be enough for each
of us that we are together –
We never separate again. –

8½

VII Calamus 32 p. 372

What think you I have taken my pen to record?

Not the battle-ship, perfect-model'd majestic, that I saw to day arrive in the offing, under full sail,

Nor the splendors of the past day – nor the splendors of the night that envelopes me –

Nor the glory and growth of the great city spread around me,

But the two ~~[illegible]~~ men I saw to-day on the pier, parting the parting of dear friends.

The one ~~who~~ to ~~remained~~ remain hung on the other's neck and passionately kissed him – while the one who ~~departed~~ to depart tightly prest the one ~~who remained~~ to remain in his arms.

9

VII. 10-356

You bards of ages hence! when
you refer to me, mind not
so much my poems,
Nor speak of me that I pro-
phesied of The States and led
them the way of their glories,
But come, I will inform you
who I was underneath that
impassive exterior – I will
tell you what to say of me,

9½

Publish my name and hang up
my picture as that of the
tenderest lover,
The friend, the lover's portrait, of
whom his friend, his lover,
was fondest,
Who was not proud of his songs,
but of the measureless ocean
of love within him—and
freely poured it forth,
Who often walked lonesome walks
thinking of his dearest friends,
his lovers,
Who pensive, away from one he
loved, often lay sleepless and
dissatisfied at night,
Who, dreading lest the one he loved
might after all be indifferent
to him, felt the sick feeling—
O sick! sick!
Whose happiest days were those, far
away, through fields, in woods, on hills, he
and another, wandering hand in
hand, they twain, apart from
other men.

Who ever, as he sauntered the
streets, curved with his arm
the manly shoulder of his
friend—while the curving
arm of his friend rested
upon him also.

10

VIII. (9) 355

Hours continuing long, sore and heavy-hearted,
Hours of the dusk, when I withdraw to a lonesome and unfrequented spot, seating myself, leaning my face in my hands,
Hours sleepless, deep in the night, when I go forth, speeding swiftly the country roads, or through the city streets, or pacing miles and miles, stifling plaintive cries,

81

Hours discouraged, distracted,
— For he, the one I cannot
content myself without —
soon I saw him content
himself without me,
Hours when I am forgotten —
(O weeks and months are
passing, but I believe I am
never to forget!)
Sullen and suffering hours —
(I am ashamed — but it is
useless — I am what I am;)
Hours of my torment — I
wonder if other men ever
have the like, out of the
like feelings?
Is there even one other like
me — distracted — his friend,
his lover, lost to him?
Is he too as I am now? Does
he still rise in the morning,
dejected, thinking who is lost to him?
And at night, awaking, think who is
lost?

Does he too harbor his friendship si-
lent and endless? Harbor his anguish
and passion?
Does some stray reminder, or the
casual mention of a name, bring
the fit back upon him, taciturn
and deprest?
Does he see himself reflected in me?
In these hours does he see the
face of his hours reflected?

12

Calamus 34 p. 373

I dreamed in a dream of a city where all the men were like brothers,

O I saw them tenderly love each other—I often saw ~~them~~, in numbers, walking hand in hand;

I dreamed that was the city of robust friends—Nothing was greater there than ~~the quality of~~ manly love—it led the rest,

It was seen every hour in the actions of the men of that city, and in all their looks and words.—

13

Calamus 43 · p 377

X

O you whom I often and silently come where you are, that I may be with you,
As I walk by your side, or sit near, or remain in the same room with you,
Little you know the subtle electric fire that for your sake is playing within me.

14

Calamus 36

p. 374

XI.

Earth! ~~My~~ likeness! Though
you look so impassive,
ample and spheric there,
— I now suspect that
is not all,
I now suspect there is
something terrible in you,
ready to break forth,
For an athlete loves me,
and I him — But toward
him there is something
fierce and terrible in me,
I dare not tell it in words —
not even in these songs.

15

To see Western Boy

XII Calamus 42
p. 377

To the young man, many things to absorb, to engraft, to develop, I teach, that he be my eleve,
But if through him speed not the ~~red~~ blood of divine friendship, hot and red—If he be not silently selected by lovers, and do not silently select lovers—of what use were it for him to seek to become eleve of mine?

16

ACKNOWLEDGMENTS

We are grateful to the staff of University of Virginia's Albert and Shirley Small Special Collections Library for access to Whitman's manuscripts (MSS 3829) of "Live Oak, with Moss" and to the University of Virginia Library administration for its generous reproduction policies.

Our thanks to the Herbert W. and Albert A. Berg Collection of English and American Literature at the New York Public Library for permission to view and cite Whitman's "Poems" note, found on the verso of an early draft of "I Saw in Louisiana a live-oak growing."

And heartfelt thanks to Steven Olsen-Smith for his illuminating scholarship on Whitman's writing process while drafting "Live Oak, with Moss," his thoughtful recommendations regarding the transcriptions of the poems included in this book, and access to his digital image of poem III's second leaf, which exposes the lines now hidden under a pasted flap. This image appears as Figure 15 in Steven's article, "The Inscription of Walt Whitman's 'Live Oak, with Moss' Sequence: A Restorative Edition" in *Scholarly Editing*, vol. 33, 2012 (scholarlyediting.org/2012/editions/intro.liveoakwithmoss.html).

The New-York Historical Society graciously allowed our access of the Victor Prevost Photograph Collection (PR 56) and our use of the Prevost photographs on pages 48–55. Our thanks to Robert Dunlap and Jill Reichenbach for their help.

And this book would not have been possible without the talents, enthusiasm, and patience of our Whitman team at Abrams: Tamar Brazis, Courtney Code, Chad W. Beckerman, Pamela Notarantonio, and Max Temescu. As Walt Whitman said, "For every atom belonging to me as good belongs to you."